Mike's Story

A Journey of Faith

Wolf Creek Mike

Eastern Passage
Wrangell Island
Alaska

wolfcreekmike@hotmail.com

Mike's Story
A Journey of Faith
Table of Contents

Mike's Story
A Journey of Faith

Why did I move to Alaska?

Many people in Seattle have asked me this question since I have been down here with cancer, and all I have been able to respond with is that I had troubles down here and Wrangell seemed to provide the ideal environment in the circumstances. It has been out of mind for so long that I have almost forgotten--except for my clear memory of not being able to trust myself not to drink and drive.

At the time I decided to move to Wrangell I was experiencing very serious financial problems in nearly all my business activities, to the point where I was effectively bankrupt. I took care of my creditors the best I was able, but in the process left the IRS 'hanging out to dry.'

The IRS was not happy. They are not used to being treated that way. The IRS claimed they were owed over $500,000. But the money they claimed I owed them, according to knowledgeable legal and accounting firms, was not owed. I told the IRS that. They did all they could to intimidate me. They assigned me a beautiful and sexy agent who gushed over all of my abilities and accomplishments. I was unimpressed. They then assigned an ex-Alaskan bush pilot to me, all in an apparent attempt to uncover some illegal activity or perhaps some hidden stash. (They eventually dropped this claim, but retained over $120,000 in penalties and interest. Later they settled for $5,000.)

Finally they set a cap on my income. I could receive $325 a month, and informed me I would not be allowed to be in business or to be a part of any business, and that anyone I might go work for would be under severe scrutiny. They also told me that I had better not get married (they'd strip my wife of *all* of her income and assets). I was to make no move without their consent. They seemed to think they had all their bases covered.

I figured I could live under a bridge somewhere on $325/mo. if I could find someone to pay me $325/mo. to live under a bridge, but I would be unemployable under those conditions.

My friend and associate, Jim Pace, who then lived in Wrangell, had previously invited me to move to Wrangell. I was pretty sure the IRS wouldn't be willing to expend the effort and money it would require to continue tracking and harassing me there, and I was right. I arrived in Wrangell on the Alaska ferry with my old van full of stuff. I rented a little shack behind the Brig Bar in what was called Curleyville. I parked my van and didn't drive it for the first year. I had no need to. With income from a business I had transferred to my friend and mining partner, Dave Tallman, I bought a 56' seiner, the SJSII, which I leased, fished halibut, and later packed salmon with. I was becoming an Alaskan.

God called me about a year after I arrived in Wrangell.

I have never felt the inspiration to put down a record of my past. I have always felt inclined to look forward rather than backward. Finally, as I am approaching the end of my life, and have as much to look forward to as ever before, I have received the inspiration to do so. The result of this inspiration is what I have titled *Mike's Story*. I pray that someone will find it useful.

I am now in what I consider to be my senior years. My senior years, in my way of thinking, did not begin until my second admittance to Virginia Mason Hospital in Seattle with a severe case of staff infection. My trademark independence and self-sufficiency were gone. I needed a 'baby sitter' just to help me keep track of my 'stuff'. I am very appreciative of those who have been willing to take the time to help me in this stage of my life.

In composing *Mike's Story*, I have, first of all, done everything I can to get the facts as absolutely as accurate as possible. The facts speak most loudly, and the facts speak for themselves. I continue to seek the help in accomplishing this. Only after getting the facts as absolutely as accurate as possible have I attempted to add literary color and humor where I thought it was appropriate.

The Ascent

As close as I can figure, the beginning of my ascent towards business and financial success began during long meditative walks in which I traveled to work and back between Los Angeles and Glendale, in 1964 or 1965. At that time, as a supposedly staunch atheist, I 'prayed' for the success I would later experience and was somehow assured would come to pass.

This was my second experience with such an epiphany. My first remembered epiphany was under entirely different and very difficult circumstances when I was 11 or 12 years old.

Somewhere around 1965 I came to Seattle to visit with my father who was living on a float-house on Lake Union. While I was there, I interviewed for a job with United Control in Redmond, Washington. After I had returned to LA they sent me an offer. I accepted and made the move. This was the beginning of my career in designing electronic circuits and systems. While at UC, I designed, according to specifications, the Rotation Go-Around Computers for the C141 Star-Lifters and the C5a Galaxies. I did quite a bit of traveling back and forth between Redmond and Marietta Georgia supporting flight tests on those systems. Under the then popular 'cost plus' practice of funding military projects, I lived 'high on the hog,' and I loved it.

My father died of a massive stroke at work in Seattle, not long afterwards.

Around 1969 I had a chance to work under one of the most senior engineers at UC, Ralph Astengo, on a Ground Proximity Warning System being developed for SAS. We both were moonlighting on the side, and both desiring to start our own companies. We combined forces on a minor consulting job for Rocket Research on the Viking probe. We hit it off and started our company together. We were 50/50 partners. That was the beginning of Advanced Technology Laboratories, Inc (ATL).

We did a lot of brainstorming trying to come up with an initial product for our new company. Our first product was a thermal flow sensor based on technology that was developed for the oil industry. We sold only a few, to our sole customer, Longview Fiber, in Longview Washington.

Tacoma Boatbuilding Company then invited us to bid on the design and manufacture of Deep Sea and Intermediate Sea Winch Control Systems. We won the $13,000 contract, rented a spare room behind a State Farm Insurance agent's office, and went to work. We divided responsibilities, with Ralph becoming director of Finance and Marketing, and I of Engineering and Operations.

We also took on a lot of consulting work helping other companies in the development of their products--truck scales, embossed credit card readers, computer-controlled drafting machines, etc. We had some failures and some successes.

Following the Winch Control contract, Tacoma Boatbuilding Company invited us to bid on Propulsion Control Systems for their PSMM (Patrol Ship Multi-Mission) vessels they had contracted to build for the ROKN. These became the springboard of our success. The Korean government bypassed their regular procurement bureaucracy and placed the management of the project in the hands of the line officers who would be taking the ships into battle with the North Koreans. These officers wanted absolutely reliable and state of the art systems. It was an environment in which I flourished.

I saw what I felt to be a serious shortcoming in the system. Bringing the turbines up to power required manual intervention by the engineers to keep the loads on the turbines fairly balanced. I took the liberty in designing into the system, an open slot which would allow the addition of a circuit-card to encourage the gas turbines (there were three gas turbines per shaft driving twin-controllable pitch propellers) to share the load with one another. The gas turbine manufacturers didn't think it would work, but I wanted the chance to try it. Later on I was given that opportunity. It worked better than anyone had thought possible. This sealed our relationship as the preferred and often sole source supplier of control and monitoring instrumentation for the Patrol Ship Multi-Mission vessels Tacoma Boatbuilding Company was successfully marketing to foreign militaries.

In 1973, while all of this was in full swing, Ralph and I incorporated ATL and issued stock. At about that time Howard Suskin, one of the founders of United Control, became aware of us and agreed to invest in our new company. He invested his $40,000, but more importantly, led us into a relationship with the University Of Washington Department Of Bioengineering headed by a Mr. Don Baker. This soon resulted in a technology transfer agreement between us where we would develop and manufacture the diagnostic medical instrumentation they were developing and experimenting with. The first such system was a pulsed-Doppler unit which augmented the echocardiographic systems that were already on the market.

We eventually began selling and delivering systems into the marketplace. We then began manufacturing echocardiographic systems, which were also developed by the University of Washington, which contained the new pulsed-Doppler capabilities. We were now going head to head with the 'big boys.'

We were forced to grow rapidly to meet the demands of the market. This move required substantial additional capital. The company was struggling financially. We decided to bring in a marketing director to expand our very profitable Marine Division, which had been our major cash cow. A division manager from Eldec, Gordon Kuenster, interviewed with me for the position. He was impressed with us and wanted in. I was so impressed with him that I met with the chairman of our board, Howard Suskin, and attempted to convince Howard that we should hire Gordon, not as Marine Marketing Director, but as president of the company. Howard had someone else in mind for that slot, but Gordon and I eventually won him over.

We brought Gordon in as president. Gordon brought in some of his key people from Eldec and the company began to turn around. Together with the University of Washington, ATL went on to develop and manufacture the ultrasound scanners that are such a large part of diagnostic ultrasound today.

In February of 1980 we sold the company to Squibb. Howard died of pancreatic cancer in Seattle shortly before the sale was finalized. I still miss him deeply.

The People

Forming the very foundation of all of that which is both good and evil in life are people. They are 'the air in which we breathe,' and form the substance of God's purposes in our existence. Many people played a very large part in all of my successes and failures. I have gotten to know a lot of good people in my life and it is they that have given life its meaning. It has been people who have given me the opportunities that have allowed me to flourish.

I cherish the people I have had the privilege getting to know personally--in the U.S. Marine Corps, in my employment, everywhere in business, and in the bars and taverns I inhabited, which were in a very real sense my home and family. I cherish the personal relationships I have had with my many associates, employees, customers, and suppliers. There are too many to list.

There is the Tallman family, who I met in the 60s through a brother who I buddied with in the Marines. I became partners with them when they needed financial help salvaging their passion and their livelihood, an Alaskan gold mine, from the courts, and from the regulators.

Then there is the founder and driving force behind the original G&G Club, a fine young. man with a passion for salvaging troubled youth. He suffered a mental breakdown over all of the problems with the new club. I brought him up to the goldmine in Alaska to get him out of that environment, and he did okay for awhile, but the temptation to suicide still haunted him. There were a lot of other people I wanted to help as well, but in the end I could not even help myself. Looking back, without God's participation, none of our efforts to help others can truly succeed.

Another was a simple supplier of prototype circuit boards, Bill Dirksen. Both he and his wife had chronic health problems. He was operating on a shoestring, often using my facilities. He was one of those fiercely independent people who, in the face of a tremendous amount of adversity, always managed to just keep going,

Instant Millionaire!

When Advanced Technology Laboratories, Inc was sold to Squibb in February of 1980 I became an instant millionaire. I had reached the top of the mountain! I would soon discover that the business and financial success I had so long sought would leave me empty and still looking for some kind of purpose and meaning in life. I had reached the 'top,' and there was nothing there. I was later to discover the book of Ecclesiastes in the Bible which seemed to describe my experience to a tee.

Anyway, I charged ahead, and continued to succeed. I founded Marcon Systems Inc., and brought into it the Marine Division of ATL, which, with a great deal of advice and support from Gordon Kuenster, I had retained in the sale of ATL to Squibb. I also founded Waubeek Mining Company, and acquired G&G Health and Racquet Club, and Novascan Corp.

The Decline

Suddenly and unexpectedly I had another epiphany. "All of this is going away." Here I am a staunch atheist and I am having epiphanies! I somehow 'knew' it was prophetic, and I also somehow knew I was the reason it was all going to go away.

I decided, at that time, to fire myself and bring in a team of a team of financial and management consultants to take over. However, their assessment was that all was well and that the future was bright. I just needed to quit worrying and continue what I was doing. But the prophecy I was given would not leave me alone.

Then it began to happen. It felt as if someone had just flipped a switch. The gold mine began to go south as record floods hit the area. The heath club I was having built was suffering severe structural failures. Marcon began to suffer from contract losses and delays, and the cash flow problems that accompany them. Around this time, Tacoma Boatbuilding, my ace in the hole, went into bankruptcy.

Waubeek Mining Company:

Record floods took out both state bridges leading to the mine requiring all personnel and supplies to be flown in and out.

Marcon:

Boeing was in the process of acquiring Marcon's systems to provide real-time monitoring of their windmill operations at their headquarters. This would have replaced the NASA on-site vans that Boeing was paying $200,000 a year to lease. At the last minute NASA denied Boeing the right to enter into the contract with us. In exchange NASA provided the vans to Boeing for free.

Bell Aerospace was in the final stages of contracting with Marcon for systems to monitor the operation and performance of the hovercraft they were building for the Navy. A company by the name of Eldec 'bought' the contract, requiring Eldec to develop a system they did not have from scratch. The Bell Aerospace program manager resigned over the decision to grant them this contract. Eldec was unable meet the system requirements, requiring that the Navy to grant them significant waivers. Had the division that handled the contract at Eldec been a larger part of the company, it would have taken down the entire company.

The president of Marine Power and Equipment was familiar with ATLs performance on propulsion control systems, and wanted me (as Marcon Systems Inc.) to supply the propulsion control systems for the new Issaqua class of Washington State ferries. To facilitate this he asked me to subcontract with the supplier of the ferries' controllable pitch propellers. Pete Weinberg, president and owner of the Propulsion Systems Inc. the supplier of the controllable pitch propellers, offered to buy my company and make it a part of his operations. I was not interested. Pete then decided to give the contract to Traffic Systems Inc., which was a supplier of traffic systems on the East Coast which he owned. The control system project manager at Propulsion Systems Inc. resigned over this decision. Traffic Systems Inc. was unable to do the job. An automobile and driver fell into Puget Sound as one of the ferries left the dock on its own. Fortunately, no lives were lost and the ferries were pulled off line. The problems were eventually resolved, but this left Propulsion Systems Inc. bankrupt and Marine Power and Equipment in danger of insolvency.

The Fall

With everything seeming to be going wrong, I brought back in the team of experts. They decided that Marcon didn't need my attention, for it was doing fine on its own. Therefore it was concluded that I hire a new president of Marcon and apply myself to resolving the problems in the other businesses. We began the search for a new president. We found the right man for the job, a man whose background showed him to be more capable and qualified than I to take the company forward, and brought him on board. It was decided that I, freed of the duties of the presidency of Marcon, would apply myself to addressing the problems with the Alaska gold mine and the health and racquet club. I did so.

However, I was receiving alarming reports from the chief financial officer at Marcron, and when I returned I found that the new president had been busy, not with the responsible management of the company, but in stripping me of the ownership of the company and personally trying to destroy me. In the time I was gone, he had run up $300, 000 in debt and deliberately saw to it that we were unable to meet payroll. He did this by funneling these and other funds to an account that was not on the books. I was able to convince Tracor Inc., a company which was looking at Marcon as a promising acquisition, to step in and take over the company. My ownership of the company was ended.

Finally, following my move to Alaska, industry giant Tracor Inc., the savior of Marcon Systems Inc., and its hope for a stable and profitable market for its products on the Mississippi River's barge lines, went bankrupt. This was one of the company's earliest programs and was nearing final approval. This program would have provided remote monitoring of the barges going up and down the river. All of my work in establishing a new product in new markets for Marcon Systems Inc went unfulfilled. I can now see that God's hand was in it all.

Other People

There were also some bad apples. We are usually able to avoid personal relationships with these, but every once in a while one sis able to slip through the cracks. For me, the one notable exception was the man I hired, on the basis of the evaluation of others, good men, to take over Marcon in my absence. He, George Davis, was easily the most despicable and immoral person I have ever known on a personal level. I can't say I didn't have reason to doubt him. His attitude toward his previous employers was one of unrestrained contempt. I even talked this over with my advisors. They thought maybe his attitude was justified. As it turned out he had a poison in his system that colored everything he did. He was overcome by the desire to build himself up by tearing others down. He was harboring bitterness, envy, and a jealousy that drove him to destroy others even without regard to whether it was of any benefit to himself or not.

He was one of two men I was committed to kill at the time I came to Wrangell. The other was an organized crime figure associated with the building of the failed health club facility This commitments was not matters of vengeance, but of personal honor. I felt each killing to be my 'sacred' duty as a man. Shortly after I became a believer the entirety of that very heavy burden was lifted from my shoulders. I then realized in whose hands these men were. I was able to see how ridiculously puny and ineffective my concept of justice was in comparison to the justice, and the mercy, of the one who has made them. I feel no hesitation in praying for them now.

Marcon Systems Inc.

Jim Pace. Came by to visit me, and spent over an hour and a half with me, while I was confined to Virginia Mason Hospital. I had a lot of opportunities to talk with Jim about George Davis and his presidency at Marcon, since moving to Wrangell, but before I became a believer I didn't want Jim in any way involved in my plans in dealing with George. After I became a believer this was all water under the bridge.

Jim shed a little light on the $300,000 debt that Marcon had accumulated and that had cost me my ownership in the company. Jim was a part of the financial team that I brought in salvage my business interests. Jim had asked me to hire him in the position controller at Marcon and I did. He was there during my absence in dealing with my other business interests.

Debbie, the secretary and receptionist at Marcon, and at that time my ex-mistress, alerted Jim that something was going on. Jim called me in Alaska and told me that I had better get back down here.

According to Jim, George had taken it on himself to over Debbie's responsibility to make the bank deposits, and to make them all personally. He then made those deposits into a separate account which was not on the books. According to the books Jim was keeping there should have been plenty of money in the bank to cover the payroll and the bills. There wasn't.

When I returned to Seattle, Debbie had been fired and Jim had moved on. George had developed and was implementing detailed plans to take over the ownership of the company for himself and a few others whose cooperation he needed. He even had reserved a small piece of the pie for me. He apparently felt I would be willing to accept something rather than end up with nothing. All he needed was my signature.

Somehow he had convinced the executives and financial team at Tracor, many of the employees at Marcon, and even the bankers, that I had taken the missing money. At that point all I wanted to do was to save the company. I requested Tracor, who was already interested in, and looking at the possibility of acquiring the company, to step in, and recommended that George be removed as president. That ended my ownership of Marcon.

Waubeek Mining Company

In or around 1981 I received a call from my old Marine buddy, Jerry Tallman. He told me that his brother Dave, who had also become my friend, needed financial help in salvaging his Alaska gold mine, which was his and his families livelihood and life's passion. This mine is located on Bird Creek near Petersville off of the Parks Highway north of Anchorage.

He and his partner had recently sold the mine for $2,000,000 to a group of California investors put together by the son of a popular Alaska Senator. But the proceeds from that sale never materialized, and the investment group had declared bankruptcy. I flew up to Anchorage to meet with Dave and his family.

Dave needed to free himself from his current partner, and would need some seed money to get him started in the coming season. Another friend of Dave's had committed the equipment necessary to set up and restart the mining operation. But, before all that could happen, his friend encountered life-threatening health problems and had to withdraw.

In this region there is a very short window of time in which equipment can be moved. We had to move fast. Fortunately there was an equipment supplier in Lynwood that had the equipment available, and because of the appreciating trend in the value of the equipment, financing was not a problem.

We were able to get the equipment there on time and Dave moved it in to the mine. I was amazed at the difficulty of moving even heavy tracked equipment over that terrain. In the process I was able to spend a lot of time at the mine, and travelling back and forth to the mine. It was a wonderful and memorable Alaska experience.

Before we got into full operation record floods hit taking out both state bridges leading into the area. Everything from that point on had to come in and out by air. I will always remember the experience of riding from Talkeetna in a Beaver airplane loaded with diesel fuel, and landing on a makeshift landing strip near the mine. I would much rather be doing this than spending my retirement as a tourist, or playing golf in the Florida Keys.

Eventually it came down to the cost of mining being greater than the proceeds received from the gold we were taking out. We were forced to shut the mine down.

G&G Health and Racquet Club.

The founder and driving force behind the health club was a young man named Daryl Theckston. He suffered a mental breakdown when his dream of a new club began to disintegrate. The man I hired to overlook the management of the construction also suddenly and inexplicably resigned.

I brought in a mman with experience in running a health club, a rough and tough biker by the name of Al Diaz. Al took charge of the operation. He also started talking to people and found out that money had changed hands and major construction violations had been 'overlooked.'

In broad daylight, and in front of witnesses, the company who owned the facility and who was in charge of the construction brought in their marked company trucks and loaded up everything I and Al Diaz owned, including our garbage and dirty laundry, and hauled it off to an undisclosed location (the man who owned this company also owned a network of storage facilities). Al called me on his way out of town. All he had left were the clothes on his back and the bike under him. He would not be able to contact me again and only wanted to wish me the best. He was fleeing for his life.

I called the police and continued to press. I hired an inspector to give me an unbiased analysis of the problems with the facility. This turned out to be of no benefit to me, for in contracting the inspection myself, none of the findings were admissible.

I was offered a 'meet' at a fairly remote bar. I received an anonymous call warning me of a rumor that they planned to take my life. I didn't go.

The policemen investigating the theft called me and told me he had located my belongings, or what was left of them, and told me where they were. He had located them in a storage unit belonging to the company that was building the health club. I would have access to them, but would have to go there alone. I was more than a little nervous! Nothing happened to me. Much was gone, including all my guns, and many records. I loaded up what was left and departed.

I took the company to court and lost, receiving only a judgment against myself for unpaid rents, rent I had refused to pay until the problems were resolved. There was no one to testify on my behalf. This ended my ownership of the health and racquet club.

Finally I got a court hearing relating to the theft of my stuff. The company put forward one of the employees of the club, a striking young lady Al Diaz had become involved with when he was manager. She was supposed to have been the one who ordered my stuff to be moved. It quickly became clear, both to the court and to myself, that she had absolutely no knowledge of even the reason for the move, or of any of the details of the move itself. But the court issued a civil judgment against her anyway.

Afterwards I tried to contact her in hopes I might get some kind of information I could use. It was futile, and I knew it. She wasn't afraid of me or of the civil judgment. She was afraid of them.

Looking back, and trying to overlook some of the people that were hurt, the whole episode seems comical--What kind of a nut case was I? It was one of my most bizarre experiences. I now realize that I was safe through the entire episode. God was not through with me yet.

As promised, I have never heard from Al. He lost everything but the bike under him and the shirt on his back. But, knowing Al, these held little importance to him. He had his freedom and his life. He was a good friend.

Novascan

Novascan was a small company near Marcon in Bellevue operated by another technical wizard like myself, Jesse Brinkerhoff. The company derived its income through consulting and contracts. The relationship between Jesse and his investors was at the breaking point, and they just wanted to recover their investment. I bought out the investors and became 73% owner of the company. One of Jesse's brothers was the owner of another company in Bellevue that was a pioneer in the development of networking systems and software. A younger brother worked for him at Novascan.

When I lost Marcon I moved the foreign military spares business that I had retained from the sale of ATL to Novascan. Novascan became a very profitable business. I let the profits accumulate in the company and we were able to get Jesse enough money for a substantial down payment on a new home. I also got him a company car. We were each able to also pull down comfortable salaries.

When I left Bellevue for Alaska I took the foreign military spare parts business with me and made it a part of another company, Novasystems Ltd., which I had formed without the involvement of attorneys and accountants as I had before. I put the company in the name of my friend and former mining partner, Dave Tallman. This company became the instrument for the continuing operation of the foreign military spares business, and fishing and packing operations as well. I operated it out of my little shack in Curleyville.

When I left for Alaska Jesse must have felt abandoned. He was! Jesse somehow got involved with another principle. They literally stripped the company of all its business and moved it across the street and under another name. I felt betrayed.

I came down and salvaged what I could of the assets--not because they were of any use to me, but at this point I didn't want him to have the use of them. I had Dave Tallman's brother repossess the company car and send it to Wrangell where Leslie and I sold it.

Wrangell
A Story of Redemption

One night, about a year after I moved to Wrangell, I was sitting in the Brig Bar with a local fisherman. Nothing was happening there, so we decided to wander down to the Stikine Inn, a waterfront bar, restaurant and dance hall. On the way we stopped in at the Totem Bar. It was empty except for a young lady drinking coffee and visiting with the lady bartender.

While I was living in Seattle, I occasionally flew up to Ketchikan to spend the weekend. The bars never closed there, and I had friends there to drink and party with. A few times I made Wrangell my destination. I hung out there at the Marine Bar , for that was where the fishermen congregated. Leslie was one of the regulars there, and definitely, not unlike me, a party animal. She would sometimes '6 pack' me with tequila. She later said I seemed lonely and broke, and so yes she did buy me drinks. When I saw her at the Totem Bar I knew it was her, but she was a different person from the one I knew then.

My fisherman friend[1] took a shine to her and wanted to take her to the Stikine for dinner. I didn't want him to get by without any competition, so the three of us went to dinner together. Leslie recently reminded me that it was she who invited me. During the course of that evening, as I sat in contemplation, wondering what had happened to her and what was going on in me, I experienced another epiphany. God, or whoever he was--I had no idea at the time--appeared to me inside all of the protective barriers I had built up over the years. I somehow knew he had every right to be there. I was astonished but unafraid. He asked of me only that I 'go along with what he is doing.' Afterwards, and before we parted for the night, Leslie looked directly at me and told me I needed to go to church in the morning. 'What church?'I asked. She told me about the Salvation Army and where it was located. That didn't sound so bad; I had heard good things about the Salvation Army. She also made it clear that I was not to sit near her or even acknowledge that I knew her. I told her I would try to be there. I had a feeling this had to do with what the person of the epiphany I had just experienced was doing.

Outside, I ran into a big burley biker type[2], and remarked to him that 'You're not going believe what I just did. A lady asked me to go to church in the morning and I agreed to do so.' 'Which church?' he asked. 'The Salvation Army, I said.' 'I've just begun going there myself. My buddy Captain Rick is the officer in charge and I am going to be there. You'd better show up or I'm going to come and find you and kick your ass.' I continued in astonishment at what was happening.

1. My fisherman friend, Bob Butts, ended marrying another of Leslie's closest friends, and a member of the SJS II crew. Kelly had been Roger Everett's girlfriend. Bob died several years ago. I have lost track of Kelly.

2. Keith Buhner is a colorful and volatile guy. He didn't show up that morning. He often challenged God to send down an angel and 'he will kick his ass.' He is a friend, and I hope a brother. We have been back in touch lately through a mutual friend.

The next morning, I showed up. When I came in Captain Rick was in the process of training his new assistant in the art of leading people to the Lord. He needed a volunteer. 'Has anyone here never made a commitment to the Lord?' I didn't know what that meant, but I sensed this was one of the things I was asked to 'go along with,' so I raised my hand. I came forward and Captain Rick began instructing his new assistant in what to do. His assistant took one look at me and refused. I never did find out why he did that. So, Captain Rick led me in the prayer himself. I didn't know what it all meant, but to me, it was a serious and binding commitment. I didn't get the sense that anyone else took my commitment that day seriously.

I didn't miraculously stop drinking and hanging out in the bars, and I did not feel drawn to do so. But it became my quest to find out who this was that came to me that night and asked me to go along with what he was doing. Of course, I also wanted to know what it was that he was doing. I struggled futilely in trying to read the Bible. It made no sense to me at all. It was a completely foreign language (religious lingo) and culture to me. But I kept going to church at every opportunity to pick up what I could. I sought help reading the Bible and talked Leslie into reading it with me, and she agreed. In my gratefulness, I fell into a sexual relationship with her. This was mostly a result of my ignorance. I just didn't know (believe) it was wrong. God continued to work with me through all of this.

Leslie and I rented and moved into the 'Green House' by the ferry terminal together. It became the crash house for anyone who needed a place to stay or a meal. We didn't have much. We were often without running water, and most often without heat, even in the middle of the winter. But we shared what we did have. Leslie met Roger there, with whom she later married and raised a family. They both entered training school and became Salvation Army officers.

One couple that sometimes over-nighted at the green house was a young lady, Julie, and her mother's 'handyman' Randy Ott. The young lady was discovered to be pregnant (at fourteen), and the handyman was suspected of being the father, which he was. Anyway, someone decided to use me as a scapegoat by telling him that I told someone else that I had seen them sleeping together. He came after me to the Salvation Army church with a hunting rifle. Fortunately I wasn't there. My mining partner Dave then loaned me his 357 magnum and I carried that with me for the next few weeks. I even kept it with me on the slime line (fish processing line) where I hung it on the wall behind me. On day the police showed up there, with Randy in tow, in an attempt to disarm the situation. Randy was later sent to prison for shooting Julie's boyfriend's bus full of holes with both of them in it.

Eventually the green house was torn down and I moved aboard the SJSII. I would come up from the harbor to the Salvation Army every morning to fix sourdough pancakes for anyone who showed up. A little girl Sonja would bring her little brother Arden down from the state housing project in a little red wagon and I would fix them pancakes.

One day Captain Rick came down to the SJS to ask me to cover for him at the Salvation Army that night. There were some temporarily homeless people who needed a place to stay and he didn't feel comfortable leaving them unsupervised. I agreed. This quickly turned into a regular homeless ministry, and I moved from the SJSII into the corps where we slept on mats on the floor.

During the halibut openers a key group from the Salvation Army, and often my mining partner Dave, would take the SJS out fishing. I had the privilege of being the skipper.

The homeless ministry was a volatile mixture of homeless men, and a few women. They often mixed with the children attending the youth center, which consisted mostly of video games and pool. But we didn't have any problems. God seemed to be overseeing it all.

I bought an old truck and distributed out of date groceries and produce that one of our local grocery stores, City Market, donated. I gave these to whoever needed or asked for it. I had enough income from Korean and Chinese military spare part business to support myself and keep the pancakes flowing.

The biggest problem we had with this ministry was with a few of the people who had been raised in church. These were among those who came to church there on Sundays and to the ladies groups during the week. They wanted us out, and their church back, and let the divisional headquarters know of their dissatisfaction with the whole thing. But Captain Rick stood firm and the ministry continued.

Somehow the national Salvation Army became aware of what was going on in Wrangell and decided to dedicate an issue of their international periodical to the ministry. Captain Rick wrote and excellent article on my participation in this ministry. In the meantime, I, shamed into doing so by all the youth that were committing themselves to the Army as junior soldiers and soldiers, joined together with them to become a soldier myself. I was uncomfortable with this decision but was assured that it was God that was calling me to do so, and that the pledge I was required to sign committing myself, my life, and every last bit of income, to the Salvation Army shouldn't be taken literally. 'If you are not hearing His call to do this, you are just not listening.'

I was soon selected as the representative of Alaska to attend a Church Growth Conference in Los Angeles. Each representative was commended for their particular service before the entire conference. I was speechless. At this same time I experienced the strangest and most beautiful period I have ever known. I awoke one morning in my hotel room overwhelmed by a peace that displaced all of the temptations and other distractions that kept me from focusing exclusively on the person and presence of the Lord. Each morning I awoke to this presence I was both astonished and grateful. But I knew this was not going to last. It was a very humbling experience. Is this a shadow of what we will experience when we are fully and finally with the Lord?

Sometime later, back in Wrangell, I found myself grumbling before the Lord. How can I continue in submission to the leadership of the Army when Your name is being blasphemed (literally) and Your leadership disparaged? God's response to me was clear. He had not called me to the Army He had called me to Himself.

I was devastated. What have I done? The Army has treated me with tremendous grace and supported me in every ministry I was involved in. I am extremely grateful to them and will continue to be grateful. But the Army is not whom I have been called to.

The pledge I made to the Army was not retractable. Nevertheless, I did the only thing I knew how to do. I wrote a letter of resignation and delivered it to Captain Rick. Basically it said that God had not called me to the Army, but had called me to Himself. It was refused. He told me it was an insult to the honor of the Army, that I was committing myself to God *through* the Army. I wrote a second letter of resignation which said basically the same thing, but was couched in terms of submission to authority, and delivered it to Captain Rick. This time, to my surprise, he accepted it and forwarded on to the Divisional Headquarters.

I expected that my ministry would be terminated and that I would be asked to leave. This was at the beginning of winter. I had sold my boat. I had no place to stay and no work prospects until the following spring. To my surprise, Captain Rick asked me to stay on, and continue my ministry. God's provision is remarkable.

When Captain Rick was transferred the incoming officers arrived with instructions to shut down all of the ministries I had been involved in. But when the new officers saw the work that was being done they took it on themselves to see that that this ministry continued.

The Homeless Ministry

One morning one of the men, Kenneth Debour (Dakota), came to me in a near panic. He and his common law wife, Toni, had been the subjects of an episode of *Top Cops* that had been featured the night before. He was the focus of a nationwide man hunt for conspiracy to commit murder. The actors had done such an amazing job of portraying Dakota and Toni's manners of speech and personalities that it was obvious to everyone that it was them. Together, we decided to face the situation head on. We went down to the cop shop and laid the situation out before the chief of police. The chief suggested we continue as normal while he followed up on the case. Dakota never was extradited. He later moved north the Delta Junction, where he died in a house fire a few years ago. He had become a very good friend to both Captain Rick and myself.

Another homeless shelter resident was a young native man named Bill. He was Captain Rick's favorite and was given his own room there. Bill was with us at least two years. He is one our few success stories. The last time I saw Bill he was working a tug Boat in the Bering Sea, a good place to stay sober and out of trouble.

When Dakota left Bill took over his common-law-wife, his boat, and his ferret. Bill eventually married Tony. Later, when Bill threatened Tony with a gun, and she went to the authorities, I went down to the boat to try to disarm the situation. At that time there was nobody there but the ferret. A few days after that episode, Bill was arrested for drunkenness and additional gun violence. Bill then moved north and got a job on a tug that only comes into port a couple of times a month. Perfect!

When Bill left Tony married another, Richard. And so it went.

Another young man, Danny from Arkansas, stayed with me for about a year. He had the most severe case of alcoholism I have ever encountered. He got his drinking under control, and eventually seemed to be doing fine. He moved north to find work. About a year later he was brought in dead from an overdose of alcohol. He was a dear friend

Another, man who called himself Ridge Runner Dave, was a radical environmentalist. His passion was to go north and be eaten by a grizzly bear. Captain Rick stuck his neck out to get him back here to help him more than once.

There were many others.

The Wrangell police did a drug bust at the local lumber mill and arrested 13 men. These became known as the 'Wrangell 13.' The police found that they didn't have enough room to house them all at the jail, so they assigned several of them to us to supervise as they did their time. These mixed right in with our homeless ministry.
There were a few fights, and a few bottles found stashed outside the premises, but overall things went very well (there were no problems associated with the Youth Group).

During this period one of the homeless men, Dennis, and I were transporting some of my stuff out to my cabin on backchannel with a borrowed skiff and motor. Shortly before we got to my place the boat took on water and suddenly rolled. I managed somehow, to throw myself up on the bottom of the sinking skiff. Dennis grabbed my legs and pulled himself up with me. There was no hope of getting to shore, and there was no hope of rescue. There was absolutely no boat traffic on the Eastern Passage that time of year and it was already turning dark. Then I heard singing. Here it is, the 2nd day of February. Sheets of ice are floating in the water nearby. The waves are breaking over us. I can't keep my teeth from uncontrollably banging together. And my friend Dennis is singing Christian hymns! Hmm. Why didn't *I* think of that? So, that is what we did as long as our strength and our voices held out.

Soon the boat sank entirely out from under us. About that time, no, exactly at that time, a boat appeared out of nowhere. One of the backchannel residents, a tug captain by the name of Charlie Gadd, had been heading to his place to pick up a pair of shoes. When he ran into hard weather he came to his senses and turned back. On the way he stopped in the cove where we were heading, to see my neighbor Paul. It was dark by that time. When he came out of the cove his course brought him right over the top of us, otherwise he could never have seen us.

We managed to get to the cove, and my neighbor had a brush fire going on the beach. I then crossed the creek to my cabin to get dry clothes. I even got a fire started. Ever try to hold a burning match in hands that won't stop violently jerking? We both got into dry clothes and spent the night in my cabin. We hiked into town the next morning.

Dennis later told me that I must have seriously injured my ribs catapulting myself out of the water into the rim of the skiff and then past that up onto the bottom of the boat. With the temperature of the water, I had a lot of motivation to get out of the water any way I could. Dennis also told me that much of the time, he was considered just letting go and letting death take him, so that his weight would not continue to press down upon me, and that I might have a better chance of survival. What chance? That is as great a demonstration of the love of Christ as I have seen. I learned much from Dennis in the time that we spent together, and especially that day, and night. He possesses a humble and contrite spirit that I can only sit in admiration of.

Dennis is now enjoying retirement with his wife Vicki and his grandchildren, in Eugene Oregon.

The first order of business for the next set of officers was to shut down all of the ministries I was involved in, and to shut them down immediately. To my surprise the strongest objections came from my friend Tim Johnson, who once hung around the Green House, and was then a purser on the Alaska State ferries. My ministry was a key part of his ministry, for it gave him a place to send the people he encountered in his work and ministry on the ferries.

I believe it was about that time that Captain Rick called me from Dutch Harbor. He wanted me to come out and help him set up a homeless ministry there. I was on my way. That opened up a new chapter in my life.

Dutch Harbor and St. Paul Island.

When I arrived in Dutch Harbor I was welcomed to a mansion on Nirvana Hill. It was just like Captain Rick to find the biggest and most elaborate home in the islands to set up shop. His church was in his home. And the church was family, not just a religious meeting.

Rick was able to get independent funding from a local processor for the homeless ministry, but was unable to get Salvation Army approval.

While I was there, I 'threw boxes' aboard Chinese ships under the Longshoreman's Union. This involved unloading bags of frozen fish off of pallets and stacking them in the holds of the ships.

Sometime later I supervised a long-line baiting operation in the harbor.

One day I ran automatic jig fishing gear on a small boat just outside of Dutch Harbor. I lack the constitution for this. I was seasick the whole time. I was amazed at how much energy it took just to keep my internal organs in place while rolling in the troughs of 12' seas.

I then went to work for a live crab processor on Unalaska Island and became their supervisor and chief crab cooker. I cooked up the dead loss for the owners and employees during my spare time. We had all the tanner crab we could eat.

I attended the interdenominational church, the Unalaska Fellowship, on the island. They had no pastor at the time, so the church was run by the elders. I loved the diversity of Christians that were represented there. However, while I was attending there, the elders brought in the 'Laughing in the Spirit' movement from Toronto, and I shared my very critical criticism of this movement with my Christian friends in Wrangell. This correspondence eventually found its way back to the church in Unalaska through a supporter of this movement who lived in Wrangell. She warned them of the 'devil' in their midst. The chief elder at Unalaska Fellowship came to me and asked me not to send a letter I had composed to this lady explaining my position, and to cease all conversation and correspondence on this subject. I submitted to his authority.

Two young couples who were part of Captain Rick' church formed a business in which they were shipping live crab to a processor in Anchorage for transshipment to Korea. I went to work with them offloading live crab from fishing vessels into totes, transporting the totes to the airport, and loading the totes aboard cargo planes. When they moved their operation out to St. Paul Island I joined them there for about the next three seasons. While staying out there and just waiting for the fleet to come in, I was able to spend a lot of time exploring the island. I wandered among the hills with the arctic foxes and the reindeer, and on the cliffs and beaches with their abundance of waterfowl and fur seals.

When Captain Rick and Sharon were transferred from Dutch Harbor to Anchorage, Roger and Leslie came out to take their place. I stayed on with Roger and Leslie at Dutch Harbor for awhile, but was asked to leave when my presence caused problems in their marriage. In a recent email Leslie informed me that it was accusations of abuse against me and others by her deranged sister that instigated my being asked to leave. It was for my own protection rather than for the sake of their marriage as I was then told.

Roger and Leslie now live in Juneau Alaska.

My Return to Wrangell

After spending some time with Captain Rick and his family in Anchorage, I returned to Wrangell. Back in Wrangell I went to work at the ferry terminal and at Wrangell Fisheries. I also I long-shored and did manual labor for a couple living 30 miles south of town for $100/month. They had offered me $10 an hour plus room and board, but I knew they couldn't afford that. I put in about 48 hours a week.

Life on the Backchannel.

As soon as I was able to retire on Social Security I did so. The A frame on a log float on the North end of the Island has been my only home ever since. I travel back and forth to town, first by rowboat to a beach head I have established. I then carry the rowboat and any gear and goods that I have up the beach to the woods. I stash my rowboat in a place I have especially prepared for it. I then travel up a trail I have made to the road system, then travel by bicycle into town. The trip normally takes about an hour and forty minutes. It is an invigorating lifestyle. It has kept me active and fit.

During the winter I do a lot of my travelling at night. I love rowing my boat under clear skies. One such night the sea was covered with whitecaps, and the fluorescence of the water was such that each wave was capped with a bright crown of light. One night the Northern Lights formed a huge spinning wagon wheel directly above my cabin. I love bicycling both day and night, especially in the snow,.

For several years before my mother died, I have, by invitation, spent the Christmas and New Year's season with her on Camano Island. I was amazed at how difficult these times would be for me. Childhood emotions don't die easily. However during these times I developed some very close relationships with brothers and sisters in Christ on the Island, and these friendships pulled me through.

In inviting Greg Summers, the pastor of Mabana Chapel on Camano Island, to take a Sabbatical at my float house, I related the time that My neighbor Paul emptied his AK47 past the front of my float-house and me, as I looked on. I confronted him as he was reloading. He was drunk. "I'm just trying to get rid of that pesky neighbor," he said. (Before I moved in next to him, he had had the cove and the entire area all to himself.)

I then had to decide whether to take him down. I knew that if I took him down he would ambush me later. I decided my best option was to walk away from the situation. As he finished reloading I turned my back on him and walked away.

For the last few years I have settled down to a pretty mundane routine. I travel back and forth to town to various church and other functions several times a week. I have become the chauffer of my friend, 94 year-young Ted Haux. I drive him to a variety of church meetings: on Tuesday mornings to the Harbor Light Men's Accountability Group, on Wednesday night to the Harbor Light Dinner and Bible Study, on Thursday morning to the Presbyterian interdenominational Men's Fellowship and Breakfast--which I have had the privilege of leading for the last few years, and to a variety of church and community functions. Ted and I pick up his sister at Senior Housing, and bring his 98 year young wife down from the Hospital's long term care, for services at the Hope Community Church of God every Sunday.

Once a month I deliver US Department of Agriculture commodities to the shut-ins and seniors of the community for the Seventh Day Adventist Church. The Seventh Day Adventist pastor gives me full use of his SUV for the day. This is one of my favorite social events.

I dedicate my mornings (5am to 8am) to reading the Bible and meditating on what God seems to be telling me through it. Journaling my thoughts often take up the rest of the morning. I have dedicated the last years of my life to the continuing development of my relationship with the One who called me. Over these past few years this has developed into a precious and intimate relationship with the Lord that I value far more than life itself. It is through this relationship that we each receive a mutual loving and intimate relationship with one another as His body, His church and His people.

This connects everything back to the beginning, back to the first epiphany I experienced as a boy. I now have plenty of people to love. God works out His will in wondrous ways.

My Faith

My faith seems to be a moving target, since God keeps stripping it down to the basics. As I approach the end of my life I find my religion becoming less and less of a factor, not more. Instead of its growing, it is being stripped to the bone.

I am not a religious person. I was not raised as a religious person, and have never felt called by God to be religious. I don't go to church for 'church,' or for the singing, or for the sermon, or even for the prayer and worship, though I earnestly endeavor to participate with my brothers and sisters in Christ in each of these things. I go to church to be with other people of faith, and with those who are being drawn to the faith.

I try to do my very best to keep in mind the fact that the course I take and the position I find myself in, are my course and position, the ones that God has called me to, and that it in no way places me on a course or in a position that is either better than or less than any other true believer's course and position. God has placed an incredible amount of diversity in His people and in His church. The challenge for us is to not let our differences develop separations between us.

I believe there are as many roads to God as there are people on earth (How's that for a controversial position?) But once we have arrived at God and Christ, as I did that fateful evening in Wrangell, there is but one way. Jesus Christ.

Within each church there are believers. Mixed in with these are often violent and blasphemous men, blatant drunks, loose women, and even sexual perverts, all struggling to overcome their handicaps. Among all of these are those who not only believe in God and Christ, but have completely dedicated their lives to that belief. Nearly all in the church profess to be believers in Christ. But few have committed themselves, their families, and their lives to living in accordance with that belief. Those represent the life of the church, which is Christ. These have given me hope.

Jos 24:14-15 14 "Now therefore fear the Lord and serve him in sincerity and in faithfulness. Put away the gods that your fathers served beyond the River and in Egypt, and serve the Lord.**15** And if it is evil in your eyes to serve the Lord, choose this day whom you will serve, whether the gods your fathers served in the region beyond the River, or the gods of the Amorites in whose land you dwell. But <u>as for me and my house, we will serve the Lord</u>."

Most of us live our lives keeping one foot firmly planted in the world. But at some point in each of our lives we must make the decision to either fully commit ourselves to God and Christ, or share the fate of all unbelievers. A committed believer is one through whom the love of God is poured out into the world. A committed believer exhibits the very nature of the Spirit God in Christ—love, joy, peace, righteousness, longsuffering, kindness, goodness, faithfulness, gentleness, and self-control.

My Tithe

Do I tithe to a church? No. Do I give at least 10% of my income to a church or to churches? Again, no. I probably fall short by about a half. My faith is not in church<u>es</u>. Have I previously giving half my income to God? Yes, in my case through World Concern. Is World Concern an integral part of God's church? Absolutely. It is certainly more so than the majority of churches, many of whom are no more than exclusive religious social clubs.

That said. I believe we must all be involved in the church<u>es</u>, as we are His church. We must not forsake the gathering together as His people. We are to love God, and, we are to love our brothers and sisters in Christ—*all of them.*

My favorite Christian author, and the one I would most likely choose to be a mentor, is C.S. Lewis. But I am not a disciple of C.S. Lewis; I am a disciple of Jesus Christ. I consider myself to be what C.S. Lewis calls a 'mere Christian,' one who is devoted to the things that have been common to all Christians throughout the ages. I am, one could say, a Christian without the trimmings.

Newspaper Articles

Victory Vignette
By A/Captain Rick Ameline

There's no satisfaction in poverty!

That's how Mike Frazier suns up his youth-raised in a home where both physically and spiritually poverty were prevalent.

Like any young men facing life from this perspective, Frazier left home to join the Marines. After being honorably discharged he went into industry. With a couple of years of college in math and physics, Frazier was able to establish himself firmly in the electronics field.

Many years of hard work and diligence, along with some "unusual luck, " produced much financial fruit, and Frazier reached a point where he and a business partner were able to sell their corporation for 67 million dollars.

Now, at lasts, security and satisfaction could be his ... or could they?

In a just a few short years all his investments turned sour, very thing that had prospered now produced failure. "It's just like someone turned off a switch, " he recalled.

Reeling from blow after blow, Frazier determined to turn his back too all the hypocrisy and corruption that permeated that lifestyle. Having no hope nor expectation, he said he saw life as a cruel joke. Hoping to "retire," Frazier moved to Wrangell, Alaska.

At closing time in a local bar, a young woman concluded her conversation with Frazier with, "How about coming to The Salvation Army for church tomorrow morning?" It sounded like an innocent enough invitation, so he accepted.

The next morning Frazier found himself in a Salvation Army meeting (complete with drums and all) wondering how he had gotten into this mess. Being "hung over" didn't help matters much.

[Sunday evening he returned at the request of his "new friends" and found the Captain speaking of salvation[3]. "Has anyone not turned their life over to Jesus Christ for new direction and guidance as we have seen here in the Scripture of John, chapter four'?" the captain asked.]

3. According to my memory and to other witnesses, everything that follows happened that same morning. It is understandable that the officer would want it to fit into the standard template, but it didn't happen that way. I *can* testify that I knew nothing of the salvation or the standard 'process' of salvation at this point. Leslie backs me up in this.

In fact, A/Captain Ameline was training his young Bible School graduate assistant in the art of *leading people to the Lord* that morning. The young man took one look at me and refused to participate in my prayer for salvation. A/Captain Rick Ameline took over from there.

Mike slowly, but with deliberation, raised his hand."Would you like to?" came the response.

At last-and he's not about to keep it secret, either. Frazier's commitment to his Savior and the corps is as remarkable.

A multitude of thoughts flooded Frazier's memory. The Holy Spirit had been at work trying to move him to this point since he was 14 years old. One of the driving forces in business had been to amass enough money to retire and help others. The conviction and guilt over this failure were overwhelming. "Yes, I would," he replied.

That decision is nearly two years old, but Frazier says there has never been any consideration given to retracting it.

The change in Frazier is remarkable. There is something about him that you notice the moment you meet him. Frazier has a quiet peace about him that tells the world he has found true satisfaction at last—and he's not about to keep it secret, either.

Frazier's commitment to his Savior and the corps is remarkable as his story. As a soldier he voluntarily rises each day at 6:30 a.m. to makes sure there are pancakes hot off the griddle at 7 for anyone who needs something hot to start the day. He serves coffee and the best sourdough pancakes in the west, along with an easy going faith that is contagious.

He holds devotions daily with all who participate our the Wrangell Corps programming for the homeless and hurting people in the island community. Every Saturday morning, Frazier and a couple of other soldiers head out to the docks to hand our free coffee and doughnuts to those who live and work on the water in this fishing community.

Daily, Frazier distributes vegetables and food donated by the two local markets to those who have need on his route. To many, Frazier seems like an angel in an Army uniform.

Of his part in life, Frazier says," 1 do simpler things now, like cleaning the floor, helping others and delivering goods to the needy." He said he is convinced that this is of greater value than the bank account he once depended on so heavily. Now he is able to do what had always eluded him in the past-help others.

The ' 'simple ' ' things that he has done have led others to eternal life, opened up a halfway house type of ministry, and led scores of people to an Army of Salvation and peace with God for the first time in their lives.

There is no satisfaction in poverty-especially spiritual poverty-but there is great satisfaction in being available to the Master for His use. Just ask Mike Frazier.

NEW FRONTIER

Published b y
THE SALVATION ARMY
Community Relation and
Development Department
U.S.A. Western Territory

business

Electronics-spinoff company diversifies in marine field

Boyd Burchard
Times business columnist

Among the innovative high-technology companies putting down roots in all sorts of diversified fields in the Northwest, it's no longer surprising to find small specialized spinoff electronics and minicomputer companies competing and serving customers across the nation and around the world.

Marcon Systems Inc., 1343 N.E. 20th St., Bellevue, is an example. The 12-employe firm makes highly sophisticated propulsion-control and monitoring systems for high-speed dually powered gas-turbine-and diesel gun boats with variable-pitch propellers built for the Republics of China and South Korea by Tacoma Boatbuilding Co.

Marcon recently designed and installed a complex, $30,000 monitoring system for the Al-In-Esk-A Sea, floating seafood processor of the 13th Regional Corp. of nonresident Alaskan natives.

It enables the skipper in the wheelhouse to eyeball TV-screen readouts of sensors throughout the converted cargo container ship and constantly keep tabs on everything from bilge levels to individual cylinder pressures to refrigeration and machinery temperatures at more than 100 critical points.

And just the other day, Marcon's president Michael D. Frazier, captured a contract to design and install $45,000 electronic monitoring systems in two 5,800-horsepower towboats being built for American Commercial Barge Lines of St. Louis, Mo.

The barging firm is part of Texas Gas Transmission Corp.'s Inland Waterways Service Division, which operates more than 50 tugs on the Mississippi River and other inland waterways.

Frazier expects this prized initial inland contract to lead to extensive American Commercial fleet conversion to the microprocessor-based, programmable Marcon performance-monitoring system.

As with many high-technology companies, Marcon is a sort of spinoff of spinoffs. Frazier, now 40, is a former marine who worked in electronics and computers with California companies and subsequently as design engineer with United Control Corp., now Sundstrand Data Control in Redmond.

He cofounded Bellevue-based Advanced Technology Laboratories, Inc, in 1973 with another ex-United Controller, Ralph A. Astengo. Today the once two-man A.T.L. has some 600 employees, is doing upwards of $10 million annually and is growing fast.

Both Frazier and Astengo have moved on separately to new ventures, but A.T.L, now presided over by a marketing-oriented fellow named Gordon B. Kuenster, is soaring on the world sales of ultrasonic diagnostic equipment and is being merged into Squibb Corp., major health services firm.

Initial A.T.L. product was a winch-control system for handling underwater equipment for an ocean-research vessel. With Frazier directing engineering and operations, the firm expanded into new marine propulsion-control and monitoring systems as well as medical ultrasonics.

The latter products, Based on university of Washington bioengineers' concepts and developed for noninvasive video-and-audio observation of people's hearts and other soft innards in action, became the main A.T.L thrust, and directors decided to sell the marine division.

Frazier, continuing as director and stockholder, of A.T.L. resigned as vice-president to set op Marcon in November.1978. He purchased the A.T.L. marine division in January, 1979 to undertake further product development with the help of some savvy associates.

A couple of fellows from A.T.L. who joined Marcon at startup included James R. Pottebaum, a performance-monitoring-system-development engineer who became chief engineer, and Edward L. Buck, former A.T.L. drafting overseer who headed up Marcon's assembly, testing, and material-control operations.

A third team member, John Cramer, described by Frazier as a "software genius," formerly was with both the Boeing Co. and Redmond-based Automix Keyboards, Inc.

Shipboard systems consisting of many individually wired gauges and alarms and "idiot lights" to monitor equipment operation and warn of malfunctions have been around a long time.

But the neat thing about Marcon systems is their ability to condense and present on one small TV-screen a multiplicity of readouts from remote sensors in a ship.

The captain or engineer or others at several viewing stations can call up on their-screens by pushbutton selection detailed information from sensors on main engines, generators, compressors, gearboxes, drive shafts, lube and cooling-systems or whatever. Potential is about 1,000 readout points.

Keys to the advance are microprocessors, collections of circuits and transistors etched on tiny wafers of silicon and designed to carry out programs, or lists of sequential instructions at great speed.

Cassette tapped programs, which can be plugged in by the operator, give the system all sorts of flexibility as compared with hard-wired systems, in which changes would require extensive rewiring.

Temperature readings, voltages, pressures, fuel flow and other information displayed across the calibrated screen by illuminated band meters enable the viewer to spot impending trouble before costly breakdowns occur.

Besides video displays, integrated systems permit information output on printers, tape recorders and even by microwave or remote shore side recording. Marcon also makes minisystems for smaller fish boats and other work craft.

User benefits, Frazier, says, include potential reduction of downtime, better preventive maintenance planning and reduction of fuel costs through more efficient operating controls.

As with many electronics advances, the new solid-states system offers more decision-making information for the dollar than older systems, takes up less space and is cheaper to install and maintain. At some crossover point, Frazier says, resultant savings to users should more than pay for its cost.

Frazier sees potential for Marcon systems in many industrial-process markets and is aiming at off-the-shelf packages with broad capabilities and programs taped for specific applications.

Growth plans? Frazier, readying a demonstration system the other day for a workboat show this month in New Orleans, said his aim is eventually to beat A.T.L.

The Seattte

Times business

Ultrasonics firm aims to replace X-ray use

by Boyd Burchard
Business columnist

Hopefully, you won't need any of the ultrasonic era and blood-flow diagnostic equipment that Advanced Technology Laboratories, Inc., (A.T.L.) is pioneering commercially in Bellevue for cardiac and vascular medics around the world.

But it just might help save your Life. And that's-not a 'bad tradeoff for your share of the Federal money which has been poured into 15 years of research and proto development at the University of Washington Center for Bi-engineering b y the National institute of Health.

The young ATL founded in 1971 by Ralph Astengo and Michael Frazier to produce new high-technology pro ducts is developing the sophisticated Ultrasound instruments under a 17-yeart technology- transfer agreement with the U. of W. signed only two years ago.

THE PRODUCT line the company has developed already is selling around the world at about a $1.5 million annual rate.

It's a series of instruments which can image valve-action and blood-flow- velocity patterns within your heart and cardiovascular system.

What's really neat is that doctors can get visual and sound readouts of what goes on in these vital–innards without invading your body.

To detect, and diagnose defective heart action or restriction in the arteries feeding your brain or other parts, for instance, it's not necessary to take the chance of injecting dye into your blood- stream or cause you discomfort.

Nor is it necessary to expose you to X-ray or other radioactive imagery systems.

THE A.T.L. SYSTEMS use the Doppler principle. Inaudible, pulsed, high-frequency sound waves are aimed and bounced off the area being examined.

The instruments measure, convert, and record the pulsed echoes for readout on a cathode ray tube and by graphic printout as [well as] by audible sound.

The pulsed readout can show how a heart valve is working or how fast blood is flowing through an artery. It can pinpoint a restriction or obstruction audibly or graphically by the difference in velocity of blood flow or by turbulence.

SINCE 1974, A .T.L. has delivered proprietary pulsed Doppler and Echo systems, priced from $20,000 to $70,000 to leading researchers and hospitals throughout the world.

Four are in use in Seattle. The Soviet Union is using A.T.L. instruments to monitor blood flows and heart-muscle movements in athletes to test endurance.

The company in late 1976 signed another technology-transfer agreement with the U. of W. for a series of hand-held ultrasound scanners. The initial peripheral-vascular scanner was in Souiub last month at the American College of Cardiology now in Las Vegas.

Medics, says Astengo, are excited by this new development for use in adult and pediatric cardiology, abdominal obstetrics-gynecology and peripheral vascular disease diagnosis.

Noninvasive nondestructive ultrasonic imagery, he predicts, is going to replace X-ray systems.

IT'S A FAR piece that A.T.L. has come in its short life. Astengo and Frazier both were United Control employees who went along with that company's sale to Sundstrand Data Control.

In 1971, awhile after Astengo invented the ground-proximity warning computer system now common on big aircraft. The pair peeled off to become their own bosses on bootstrap financing and to find new needed products to which to apply their versatile talents.

They got a $10000 Tacorna Boat Co. job to develop a winch control, then a $150,000 contract for an electronic propulsion-control system for fast Korean gunboats.

This boosted their capital, and new electronic marine-control systems
still are a division of the business headed by Frazier as vice president.

THEY GOT INTO medical electronics after Howard H. Suskin, one of the founders of United Control and now chairman of A.T.L., became a stockholder and active adviser who steered them that way.

The present 15 stockholders and board members and financial and clinical advisers of the 35 employee firm include recognized authorities in their fields.

Among them are Robert M. Bridgforth, Jr. a founder of Rocket Research Corp., Samuel N. Stroum, owner of Shucks Auto Supply and chairman of Laser Link Corp., Jack Goodfellow of Futura Corp. and Jerome Schulin, attorney.

A key consultant is Donald W. Baker, assistant director of engineering at the U. of W. who was responsible for the basic design of the pulsed Doppler.

GORDON B. KUENSTER, broadly experienced marketer and business planner who once was with The Boeing Co., joined A.T.L. as president and chief operating officer in January as the firm turned the profit corner.

Kuenster's projections for A,T.L. now "climb of the chart," with next year's sales to hit $2 million. He estimates that with 30 per cent of the domestic-market share, alone, in its field, A.T.L. would be doing $500 million annually in 20 years.

Astengo, 41, now vice president and "the bridge between engineering, finance and marketing," says "some big companies want to buy us out. But we're inclined to stay right here and eventually buy them out."

A stated company objective is "to qualify A.T.L. for public ownership within five years."

Bellevue
Firm Merged
With Squibb

The takeover of Advanced Technology La oratories Inc. of Bellevue by New York - based Squibb Corp. has been completed. The official merger date was Feb. 1.

As previously announced, each share of the Bellevue firm's common stock was exchangeable for a half share of Squibb, a giant pharmaceutical and cosmetics company. On the merger date, there were more than 2.48 million outstanding shares of Advanced Technology.

The Bellevue company manufactures ultrasound scanning equipment in the diagnosis of a wide range of medical problems and diseases.

Richard M. Furlaud, Squibb chairman and chief executive, said the merger, first reported several weeks ago "would be a rewarding one for all concerned."

Philips Medical Systems to acquire American ATL Ultrasound

Eindhoven 11 September 1998 *Philips Medical Systems (PMS), the Dutch leading manufacturer of medical imaging devices and software for hospital radiology departments and laboratories, has paid about 800 million dollars to acquire the Seattle based company ATL Ultrasound. This surprising business transaction will turn PMS into an international top player, particularly in the field of ultrasound applications, according to the Automatisering Gids. Ultrasound indeed constitutes a huge market potential. In the United States, a yearly amount of nearly 100 million dollars is spent on ultrasound techniques for female patients alone, whereas the market annually increases with 12 to 15 percent.*

ATL (Advanced Technology Laboratories) is a major provider of diagnostic systems and is highly specialized in digital broadband ultrasound devices and software. In this particular domain, PMS practically had no part in the growing market development up till now. In the years to come, the Dutch hospitals plan to spend hundreds of million guilders to digitize their radiology departments. An increasing number of medical experts, including cardiologists, urologists, and pathologists, are already applying ultrasound techniques to facilitate the process of diagnosis.

PMS will integrate all products and services of ATL Ultrasound into its own product assortment. ATL has realized an annual turnover of 430 million dollar in 1997. Globally, about 2600 co-operators display a dynamic activity in more than one hundred countries in Europe and the United States. For Philips spokesman Paul Smit, this means reason enough to believe that the acquisition will offer PMS important chances for growth within the Dutch marketplace. In the Netherlands, the PMS turnover amounts to between 15 and 20 million guilders. The company has subsidiaries in more than one hundred countries all over the world.

In the past, ATL has been partnering with Kodak's medical division to further the development of image management and to promote the use of the DICOM (Digital Imaging and Communications in Medicine) standard for medical imaging technologies. This activity has been fully taken over by Kodak now. Nevertheless, the Kodak and ATL systems are perfectly compatible thanks to the DICOM standard, according to PMS. In Dutch health care, there exists a growing tendency to apply state-of-the-art systems from abroad. Earlier this year, PMS decided to replace its self-designed laboratory system Labosys with software developed in the United States. The *Virtual Medical Worlds Magazine* has reported on this evolution in the article Philips Medical Systems reseller in Benelux of Sysware's PowerLAB.

Leslie Versweyveld [Medical IT News][Calendar][Virtual Medical Worlds Community][News on Advanced IT]

Santa Barbara, CA. December 18, 2000 - Green Hills Software today announced that its MULTI IDE and the ThreadX® Real-Time Operating System (RTOS) have been selected by ATL Ultrasound to develop software for a next-generation broadband digital beam former that yields clearer ultrasound resolutions. Application software developed using MULTI will run on Intel i960 and Motorola PowerPC processors under the ThreadX RTOS.

More On ATL Ultrasound
ATL Ultrasound is a worldwide leader in the manufacturing, distribution and service of diagnostic medical ultrasound systems. ATL Ultrasound is a part of Philips Medical Systems, a leading supplier of diagnostic imaging systems and related services worldwide that employs more than 11,000 people in more than 100 countries. Royal Philips Electronics of the Netherlands, one of the world's largest and most innovative electronics companies, acquired ATL in 1998. For more information on ATL Ultrasound products, please call 1-800-982-2011. http://www.atl.com.

What the Memos Reveal About the Issaquah
SHELBY SCATES

The vessel Issaquah turns up like a tough young con tattooed "BORN TO LOSE," the symbol of trouble in Washington state's ferry system that the state Senate now says it will investigate.

The Issaquah, the only one of six new ferries contracted between the state Department of Transportation and Marine Power and Equipment Company that is now operational, keeps running into things.

No one has been hurt, although damage to the ferry dock in West Seattle is running up the cost of that initial $105 million contract. The fact that there may be casualties from this misguided nautical missile has prompted two stunning confessionals by persons intimate with the Issaquah.

Jim Wright, the fast-talking industrial salesman, and Mike Frazier, a computer whiz who speaks the language of electronics, put together the original propulsion control package for the Issaquah and sold it to Marine Power.

It was a marriage of mechanics —a variable pitch propeller — with an analog computer, state of the art in 1977, say Frazier and Wright, but already tested on the systems they installed on 16 gunboats.

What Marine Power wound up installing, say Wright and Frazier, is a micro-processor computer, Untested and they claim, outside the specifications laid down by the state for a propulsion control system.

Their motives for "going public" have been questioned by Pete Wennberg, the crusty president of Propulsion Systems, Inc., subcontractor for the ferries" propulsion system. Wright used to work for Wennberg until he called attention to the switch in computer controls to the people who are supposed to supervise this contract for the state. When he found out that Wright had blown the whistle, Wennberg fired his salesman.

He now hints that Wright and Frazier had a vested interest in undermining his contract

That's hard to believe. Wright waited two years to make his information public and then with great reluctance and in the presence of his attorney. He's worried about losing other industrial customers as a result of this notoriety.

"My only vested interest is that I am afraid someone will get hurt if I remain silent," he said. As an original' participant in the contract, he also feared personal liability if the worst occurred.

Frazier was even more sluggish in surfacing. He did so only in response to direct questions.

"I got dragged out," he says of his interview with two newsmen last week. No doubt the state Senate committee probing this matter will drag him further.

But if they stop with Wright, Frazier, Wennberg and Marine Power's family Woeck, the job of the Senate inquiry won't be half done.

There may be greater questions about this contract. One former state legislator has already talked openly about kickbacks in connection with it — a charge that attracted a libel suit.

First things first. Nothing is more important than the safety of ferry passengers. This hinges on the reliability of the propulsion system. And on this reliability hangs the credibility of the state ferry system.

Senate investigators need to talk with engineers hired by the state to supervise this troubled contract. Most work directly for Larry Glosten and Associates in Seattle or Glosten's subcontractors.

Their silence in this matter is burning. You can't blame them. To talk publicly is to lose their jobs. But neither can the state, which is funding these jobs, leave them in troubled silence.

Glosten will not return the telephone calls of newsmen. He is known to have said, however, that we should check the records.

I did this last week: test memos, number 25 and 26, on the ferry Issaquah. As far as a layman can judge, they are most significant for what they don't show.

Reports on virtually every test on the vessel's propulsion system are signed by one of the engineers working under Glosten, most of them by R.B. Grant. However, three key test reports on the vessel are not signed by the State's independent supervisors of the contract.

These are: The dockside test on June 20,1980, which alleges the propeller goes from "full feather" to "full astern" in 24 seconds. It is signed by John Strada, the DOT engineer in charge of the project.

• The 16-knot crash stop test made on the Issaquah on May 18, 1980. It claims the vessel stopped in "49 to 47 seconds." There is no signature on this report by anyone.

• The 16-knot crash stop made on June 23, 1980. This time the report says the vessel went from 16 knots to dead in the water in 48 seconds. But on the last page where it asks "approved by," there is a blank space. No sign-off. "That's an oversight," insisted the DOT'S Strada, "just a clerical error — a little clerical problem. I'll vouch for that data. I was there."

OK. But will Glosten, the independent supervisor, vouch for these reports and the reliability of the vessels? I don't know. He isn't talking to newsmen. Maybe he'll tell the senators. It's past time they found out.

Seattle Post-Intelligencer THE VOICE OF THE NORTHWEST SINCE 1863
VIRGIL FASSIO Publisher
WILLIAM ASBURY, Editor
JOHN REISTRUP, Managing Editor
RICHARD J. TRENT, General Manager
WILLIAM R. COBB, Business Manager
JOHN de YONGE, Editorial Page Editor

A Personal History

The Mike Behind *Mike's Story*

I was born on May 30, 1939 in Walla Walla, Washington, as Michael Daris Frazier. I was raised in Walla Walla, Spokane, Lake Pend Orrville, and Illahee and Gilberton on the Kitsap Peninsula. I was a lousy child, a lousy student, a lousy young man and a lousy Marine. There may be reasons, but there are no excuses. I will spare the sordid details of a lonely young man who was a peeping tom. I will include one early experience because it may shed some light on my future behavior, and point to how really bizarre my first epiphany was.

My life is an open book now. Why and how God brought me through all of this unscathed and finally into His kingdom is a mystery I have been unable to fathom.

Whiskey Rock, Pend Orrville
The beating
When I was about 4 years old my family moved to Whiskey Rock on Lake Pend Orrville (Pond-or-ay) where my dad could get a job that would excuse him from the draft. While we were there, both my father and mother worked, so I was placed in a day care center. The very first day the teacher had a display table set up to impress the parents. The table was covered with a paper sheet, and on that table were some classroom materials including a hand held paper punch. One of the kids (or perhaps the teacher herself) had taken that paper punch and punched the edge of the paper sheet with it and left it hanging. Each child repeated this as they took their tour of the table. I did as well. After we had been seated the teacher 'discovered' this infraction and called the class to attention. 'Who punched the paper sheet and left the punch hanging?' No one responded. Then she said it was OK, she wasn't going to punish anyone for it. She just wanted to know who did it. I raised my hand.

She came and grabbed me and took me back into the coat room, just out of sight of the class. She then took a coat hanger and beat me with it severely as I screamed. She took me back and stood me before the class. 'What do you say?' I had no idea of what to say for I had no idea why I was being beaten. She then took me back in the coat room and repeated this process again, and again, and again, and again. I do not know how long this went on but it seemed to go on forever. Finally she stood me in front of the class one more time, but this time said 'tell the class that you are sorry.' I think I said 'I am sorry.' Anyway she sent me back to me seat where I tried to look like I was sitting down. I suspect she had a very obedient class from that point forward.

I did the best I could to hide my marks. When they were finally discovered all I remember is that I lied about them.

This one experience had a lasting effect in the way I viewed teachers, and authority, and my peers.

My family:

Our father had a severe drinking problem. I have often believed it was more the fault of my mother than his. When he was not home and in his place (under her authority) according to her schedule, my mother would throw a tantrum when he did come home. Who would want to come home to that? Better to have a few more drinks before 'facing the music.'

Finally there was very violent blow up with my mother striking my father and throwing anything she could get her hands on at him. He left.

At this time I had setup a shelter under a tree overhanging the beach where I slept and made 'sheepherder's bread' over a small fire. It was a very comfortable place to be.

When our father returned home for the final time, drunk, he was severely beaten by two my mother's boyfriends as my brother Richard and I looked on. At this point I felt as if I was locked in a trance. I could not believe my lack of response in defending my father. I knew I had just lost my father forever, and that I fully deserved to lose him.

My First Epiphany

My first epiphany came in the form of a bizarre inspiration that moved me to declare to my mother that I had chosen to love people. It was a direct slap in her face, and I knew it. I expected her to hit me, but instead she just walked away. I had declared myself to be absolutely worthless. The relationship we *did* have was severely damaged. She would not even say Hi to me after that. I left a time-capsule type note reminding myself of this, and stating that I should 'never ever have anything to do with that woman again.' A mysterious aspect of my first epiphany of memory is that in my bold declaration of my decision to love people, I had no people to love. I was socially isolated and lacked social skills. I was a loner. I would have to wait until much later to exercise that love. My greatest fear as a child was the fear of dying alone and unwanted. That is no longer a possibility.

Not long before my mother was placed in a nursing home, she sat my brother and me down and explained how much she had sacrificed for us. She told us that we could have no idea how much of a hell it was to be a young woman and not have access to either birth control or abortion. If she could have prevented us, she would have. If she could have aborted us, she also would have done so. But, neither was available under the laws of that time.

She did have us (obviously!), and she did raise us, much of that time as a single mother and without any help from our father. We both owe her much. She is proudly known as being a radical feminist before Feminism became popular. I owe my life to Feminism's taking so long to come along. I am saddened that it has now done so.

Run Away

I believe I was in the middle of my junior year at Central Kitsap High School in Silverdale Washington, when I felt I had taken all I could take and would take at home. I resigned from the National Guard and checked out of school. I stashed my guns and some keepsakes under an abandoned building. I left a note saying I was going to join my father in California (I had no idea where he was), and took off that night. I made it as far as the other side of Bremerton, but made the mistake of walking through an industrial area that was patrolled by the police. A police car showed up, and I was stopped and searched. I had a few cans of soup in my possession and was wearing at least two layers of clothes. They arrested me on suspicion of burglary, and then received at report of an armed runaway. They had me red handed.

I was taken to juvenile detention and spent the next few days there. I had no visitors. I was given an appointment with juvenile psychiatrist at the facility. He spoke with me and determined two things. I was 'near superior' in intelligence and that I needn't worry about 'losing my mind' for I had 'my head screwed on too tight.'

After a few days my mother and her current boyfriend came and retrieved me. They took me home, but since I was an obvious flight risk, they moved me into the boy friend's mother's home in town, where she and her neighbors could keep an eye on me, and where I could help her with her chores and her garden.

I was later taken home, where my father, who had somehow found out about me, came to invite me to come and live with him in Seattle. I happily accepted. My father had a $7 a week hotel room in the University District in Seattle. He kept a pot of stew on the stove which every night he would add to. It was great! I have often tried to duplicate that stew, without success.

My dad then married his friend's daughter, Sybil Hull, so that I would have a better place to live and a place to attend school. We moved into the basement apartment at 2323 Boylston Ave, N. in Seattle. I completed High School at Lincoln High School in Seattle, and received my diploma. From there I joined the Marines on November 10. 1957.

The Marine Corps

I started out in MCRD boot camp as squad leader, but was removed because of my bad attitude (toward the drill instructors). I made expert rifleman in boot camp, the top shooter of the platoon. I later received honors and letters of recommendation from Marine Generals and Navy Admirals for my scholarly achievements. But I should have received prison time and a dishonorable discharge for my attitude and behavior. How I made it through I do not know. In the Philippines, Navy short-arm inspectors recommended my dishonorable discharge on *moral* grounds. I didn't even know what they were talking about.

Memphis Tennessee

I completed the Navy's electronics training program in Memphis. I graduated at the top of my class and was given the choice of specialties. I chose air-launched guided missiles, which involved working on Sparrow (radar controlled) and Sidewinder (heat seeking) missiles.

My MOSs (Military Occupational Specialties) were guided Missile technician and Radar technician. But my specialty in the Marine Corps, as anyone who knew me can testify, was climbing fences. I had a natural tendency to always be living on the very edge of destruction, physically, legally, and morally. I was a rebel.

El Toro, California

I met Jerry Tallman, my gold-mining partner's brother, on the base as we were each on the road with our gear on the way to check in at our new quarters. Jerry was to watch our gear as I went to arrange transportation. When I returned he was gone and all my gear was in the ditch. I knew I was going to have to kick his butt, but I wasn't sure how I was going to do it, since he was much larger than I. An ambush would have to do. But before the opportunity presented itself we somehow had became friends.

At El Toro, I learned to climb fences. My superiors knew about my escapades, for word got around. But they were willing to turn a blind eye to them, as long they didn't affect my work, and as long as I wasn't caught .

.

Atsugi, Japan

In Atsugi I played cat and mouse with the Japanese guards, who patrolled the perimeter and fence which passed through a valley between the Navy and Marine bases. This valley supported the local truck farms, and was territory that was fully off limits. It was rumored that someone was seen climbing the fence in suit and topcoat in broad daylight. I had a mistress and a rented house in town.

Cubi Point, Philippines

I did not even attempt to go over the fence here. There were just too many hazards. I was forced to behave myself (to a point) so that I could get authorized liberty.

While there, Jerry Tallman, I, and a couple of others were granted leave to tour Hong Kong and Kowloon on the Chinese mainland. We stayed in a hotel in Hong Kong. One day we went to Kowloon, I became separated from the rest of the guys, as was my habit, and they may have done the same. Anyway we all missed the last ferry back to Hong Kong. I caught a ride on a skiff across the channel, and the others apparently did the same. Anyway we all ended up in the same little bar in Hong Kong. Someone decided we should take some ladies (prostitutes) back to our hotel room, so we loaded up and went back there. Things quickly and predictably went down-hill from there—a flooded bathroom etc.

Atsugi, Japan

I began getting liberty again, and my friend Jerry and I often traveled by train to Fujiama, where I had a little bootlegging operation in Scotch whiskey, until the authorities got wise to me.

Ping Tung, Taiwan

At Ping Tung Taiwan nobody was given liberty. A couple of other Marines and I tried to bluff our way through the main gate, but were refused exit. There was no fence around most of the base, but rather a dirt mound that separated the base from the surrounding farmland.

I 'took' liberty the first time with a Chinese Marine sergeant I been introduced to, who sold the Marines a plumb liquor that he made on a small orchard just inside the base. We went over the mound but were quickly challenged by a guard. He took off zig-zagging through the rice paddies with me right behind him. The rice paddies were knee deep in mud and feces. We zig-zaged so as not to give the sentry a clear shot. Supposedly their practice was not to shoot unless they had a sure shot as they had to give an account of every bullet expended. I never did find out whether this was true or not. We made it. We had no trouble on our return. Once I knew the route I took liberty on my own.

One time I took another Marine with me and we went to the nearby city, Taipei. We were riding in a pedicab and passed two Marine MPs! I couldn't get the pedicab driver to go fast enough so I sent him back to my seat and took over. I did all right until I came to a corner. I tried to lean it around the corner but it wouldn't lean. I ended up running it up on the sidewalk and into a shop. I don't know whether the MPs were pursuing us or not. I can imagine them laughing too hard to bother with the chase! I had a hard time living that one down.

Once, near the end of our tour, as I was returning to the base alone, I Heard a commotion above me on the other side of the mound. At sunrise the next morning there were shots. They had caught a sentry asleep at his post. The Taiwanese considered themselves to be in a state of war with the Chinese mainland.

El Toro, California

In nearby Santa Anna, Jerry Tallman and I joined some friends who were hanging out at a local party house. This party house was owned by a single lady, who I later became involved with.

While at El Toro, I completed the Navy's Radar school along with a sergeant named Charlie Millard. Charlie was a severe alcoholic who claimed Rakkatan as his god. He was a good friend of both Jerry and I. Charlie and I both came to class every morning with severe hang-overs. The Navy instructors were disgusted with us. But, to their astonishment, we both did well. I missed only two questions out of the 100, and those two questions were immediately removed from the tests as being misleading. I broke the record my sergeant major in maintenance had been trying to break for many years, and so my liberty was restored. Before that I had been going over the fence and along a grove of trees to get to town.

Charley married a good friend of Jerry, his girlfriend Joyce, and I. Linda was roommate of Joyce, and was also a 'lady marine.' We lost track of them after Charley was sent to Vietnam. We suspect that Charlie was killed there.

San Clemente Island ('Goat Island'), off the coast of California

It was time for me to learn how to drive. I volunteered for a course in driving six by six's (military transports). It was assumed that everyone there already knew how to drive, so I made it through with classroom work and written tests. I called it my 'Sears and Roebuck' license.

One night we were to drive our trucks to a Navy base where we would take a jeep carrier to this island off the coast. I knew we were going to have to travel through Los Angeles to reach the base, and I knew I couldn't drive. I also knew my back up driver could. So, I proceeded to get drunk, so that he would be sure to take over. When my buddy arrived he climbed into the passenger side and immediately passed out. We were both drunk.

As we left, I gunned the truck and managed to make it off the base and onto the highway going north. The guys behind me were amazed that I managed to keep it on the road. I made it as far as Sunset Boulevard in LA before the cooling system blew. We were towed the rest of the way.

The next morning I had to drive the truck backwards up a 30 degree ramp to the top of a jeep carrier. The lieutenant told me to just keep the wheel straight and gun it until I was told to stop. Nuts with that! I leaned out the door and gunned it almost falling out. But I made it better than most of the others so this infraction was overlooked. Perhaps the lieutenant thought I knew what I was doing. I didn't lose my chance for liberty.

Once I was there I stole a jeep out of the motor pool, and another marine and I drove to the CPO club on the island. Somehow the chiefs there felt obligated to put up with us, so we got drunk and made it back without being caught.

There were abalone on the rocks on the beach there, and we learned to harvest them with entrenching tools (to the dismay of Fish & Game). We fried them in crackers and butter in a cave above the beach. They were delicious. We also bought pizza from the cooks on duty. We had a great time.

Then it came my turn for liberty. It was our standard practice for the man who had liberty to make booze run to the mainland. We were flown to the mainland in a small plane. On my return I found that the tent I had been staying in, tent 13, was disbanded. The guys there had all gotten drunk, knowing that I would soon return and replenish their stocks. They has supposedly staged a mini-rebellion, at least according to the sergeant that came in to break up the party. That just doesn't happen in the Marines! Everyone received captain's mast, including Jerry and Charley. The only thing that saved them was the cowardice of the sergeant. He had retreated rather than enforcing his authority. He received the more severe sentence.

The other driver drove the truck back to El Toro from there.

Los Angeles

I received an honorable discharge from the Marine Corps, three months early to attend LA City College in Los Angeles. I blew this opportunity. My attention span was such that I was unable to learn anything that did not hold my interests. The only grade I received higher than a C was an A in calculas.

I went to work on the graveyard shift at nearby Litton Industries in Beverly Hills. I rented a room near the college in LA and spent most of my spare time in the Monica Bar on Sunset Blvd. I drank my way to work and drank my way home. This left no time for study.

Another Booze Run

While visiting the Sana Anna party-house one weekend, Jerry and I, and a couple of other guys, decided to make a booze run to Tijuana. When we got there we loaded up the trunk of my old Studebaker with gallons of Mexican Rum and Tequila. I insisted we not even bother trying to conceal them since if we got caught, and we probably would, I wanted to play dumb. When I drove back across the border, I looked the agent straight in the eye and he passed us through without searching our car.

I returned to work and school in LA, but a wild party and bloody fight took place at the party house that brought in the police. When all the untaxed booze was discovered, the FBI also became involved. The guys who were involved spent the night in jail, and afterwards underwent questioning by the Feds. The FBI never did catch up with me, but they banned my Studebaker and I from ever crossing the border again.

The Monica Bar

When my friend Jerry got out of the Marine Corps he joined me in L.A., and we got a bigger apartment. We both worked at Litton Industries in Beverly Hills. His girlfriend, the 'lady Marine,' Joyce, would visit us and cook for us on weekends. The Monica Bar was our home, and an old couple who owned the bar, in a sense, became our adopted parents.

Working the graveyard shift made me a regular pall bearer for those died who attended the Monica Bar. This was the only way I would spend time in church. Jonny Irish (John Campbell), a Catholic, was a good friend and drinking buddy of ours there. He came in one morning, ordered a seven-up instead of his usual, and asked to be driven to the hospital. He was dead before he arrived there. Another lady was run down crossing the street as she left the bar. A few others died of natural causes..

Jerry eventually married Joyce and they moved to Seattle, where I joined him later.

When Jerry and Joyce and their two daughters later moved from Seattle to Ketchikan, they got as far as the Canadian border and were not allowed to cross for the lack of the necessary cash. I had to dig up some money and meet them half-way so they could continue their journey. I ended up following him again, this time north to Alaska.

> Jerry and Joyce had two daughters. Jerry is presently living with a new wife in Ketchikan. He stopped and visited me at Virginia mason while I was there. Joyce is living with her new husband in Mt. Vernon.

After Jerry left, I became involved with a Western dancer and her friends, who were a part of the entertainment circles of the theaters and cocktail lounges of Santa Monica. One night while driving my 'squeeze' and another couple home, I was stopped by the police. I got out of my car and went back to find out what they wanted. The two cops treated that as an aggressive act and arrested us.

Once in my cell one of the arresting officers presented me with a large perfumed bag of pills that I had allegedly stashed underneath my seat. I spent the next five days in jail in Santa Monica. Once this period was completed they were required to transfer me to the LA jail, where I got my first phone call. I contacted a friend, Jerry Itkoff, who was able to bail me out. The other guy, and entertainer, was later released and fled the state.

My friend, Jerry Itkoff, knew an attorney, whom he contacted on my behalf, and we finally got a court hearing. I then had the opportunity to confront my accusers and called them the unprincipled liars that they were. I also cornered the Public Defender in the hallway outside of the courtroom (to the consternation of my attorney), and advised him as to what questions to ask me. Based on this testimony the case was dropped. I later found out that one of the cops had been dating my then 'squeeze.' She had pushed him down a flight of stairs when he came uninvited to one of her parties.

A short time later these same two cops attempted to pull me over as I was leaving after a night in Santa Monica. This turned into a high speed chase (with my little Studebaker no less). I had just made it across the border into West LA (by about 20 feet!) when they forced me off the road. Fortunately for me, at about that same time, two LA motorcycle cops appeared. The Santa Monica cops dismantled my car, but were unable to get away with planting any drugs. It quickly became obvious to the LA cops what was going on and they became my defenders. All I got out of this was a speeding ticket.

After this, one of the 'ladies' who attended the Monica Bar moved in with me. She had a car which much improved our situation. But then her husband eventually came up from Texas and collected both her and the car, which was my only transportation then. I thought that was pretty narrow of him!

Then another lady from the MonicaBar, Patty, moved in with me, and talked me into marrying her. It didn't much matter to me.. When I got a better (more challenging) job with Electronic Specialties in Glendale, I began my meditative walks back and forth to work.

She and I eventually moved into a house in Burbank with her two daughters. While I was working she was spending my money in the bars and on other guys.

When I took the Job at United Control in Redmond I expected to leave her behind, but she insisted on her and her two daughters coming with me. We packed up everything and moved .

The situation didn't improve between us there. She got involved with a church there, and was hustling money from the pastor by telling him I was abusing her and her two daughters, and was not allowing her any support money. This is one instance where I was innocent of all charges! The pastor came to me and found out what was going on. He immediately cut her off from all assistance. I finally was able to divorce her.

Shorty after that this pastor brought some of his people from his church over to my place and they cooked me a delicious meal. He told me that all I needed to do to join his church was to sign a contract with him to buy the very expensive set of pots and pans they used to cook the meal! I remember him and an associate of his reciting what must have been the gospel to me then also, but I was determined not to hear it.

I later married again. This marriage lasted six years, no thanks to me. It was during this time that I became co-founder of ATL Gladys' sister Esther became our first employee. She had worked for United Control as a lead assembler in their Model Shop. Gladys, Esther, and one of her other sisters, Irene, and a niece, Kathy, also came to work for us and continued with me at Marcon.

The Development of My Faith

The Culture of Hatred

This culture of hatred that drives much of our politics today is the same culture of hatred that was so prominent when I was a boy. It is rooted in the hatred of anyone who might stand in the way of the people's revolution--the international collectivist state, or whatever the latest political, social, eugenic, or religious movement might be.

In speaking with my mother's friends during my visits with to her, I was told that that The Soviet Union was the model for all future governments, and that the only thing that Stalin did wrong was his delay in bringing race and gender warfare into the mix soon enough. They told me that the *reason* the Soviet Union failed was that it was resisted. What this says is that it was the fault of the people whose necks were under the fascist boot of their ideology and organization, and not the fault of the ideology and organization itself. This same philosophy could apply to any number of fascist or religious ideologies. Most of these people call themselves Liberals.

We find the ideology behind each of these to be the very worst of the depravity of the nature of man coming to the surface. The international collectivist ideology, in particular, has resulted in the greatest slaughter of innocents that has ever occurred in the history of the earth. It is making a strong comeback today.

In observing the 'Seattle' liberals it has become apparent that they are "bombs ready to explode." Unfortunately, every major city in this country, Europe, the Middle East, and elsewhere are full of "bombs ready to explode." The twenty-first century could easily make the twentieth-century look like a century of peace.

The Development of My Faith

When God appeared to me that night in Wrangell, He asked only that I go along with what *He* was doing. He was bringing me gently into His will. Had He attempted to impose upon me the full dose of the laws that the church has acquired and developed over time, at that time, as the church is inclined to do, I could not have endured it. I would have immediately given up and turned back to the life in which I had lived--a life which leads only to death.

In coming under His will I was, first of all, acknowledging Him and embracing His nature—the nature of righteousness, purity, justice, and mercy love, joy, peace, longsuffering, kindness, goodness, faithfulness, goodness, and self-control. This was a nature that I had once sought diligently, and found that this world is unable to offer it. And I certainly couldn't find it in me!

This stage or phase of my faith represented the incredible beauty of an encounter with God, an epiphany. Once I was given this taste of God and of His nature, and only then, was I asked to take on the difficult things--the participation in the overcoming of and death of the sin and of the nature of that sin in me. At the time, the nature of that sin defined who I was. I would have thought that adultery, fornication, and drunkenness, uncleanness, lewdness, idolatry, sorcery, hatred, contentions, jealousies, outbursts of wrath, selfish ambitions, dissensions, heresies, envy, murders, drunkenness, revelries, and things like these would have been the first among the things I was to overcome. But I was wrong. God had deeper and more serious issues than these to address.

My Introduction to the Church

When I was introduced to the church, I found that the obvious sins, the blatant ones like these, were not allowed to be seen in the church. The sins I did encounter in the church were much more insidious than these, and much, much more deadly to the body. These sins were self-centeredness, selfishness, self-righteousness, spiritual arrogance, and hypocrisy. Though the people within the church seemed to be either unaware of these sins, or unwilling to face up to them, their duplicity was apparent to most of the people outside of the church. These were often the dominate factor driving the men and women who pressed themselves upon the church as its spiritual, moral, and political leaders. These men and women lifted up so-called 'holy' hands to God and spoke grand prophecies 'from God.'

As I became introduced to Jesus Christ, I was alarmed by the number and influence of these 'bad apples' in the church, both historically and today. I have witnessed behavior in the church that would never be tolerated in any of the bars and taverns that I once inhabited. As one who is of the church, I personally, deeply, and sincerely apologize to those who have been hurt by them.

But, of course, these 'bad apples' are also in God's hands. God is not challenged by our unfaithfulness. He is there for those of us who will remain faithful.

> **Ro 3:3-5 3** What if some were unfaithful? Does their faithlessness nullify the faithfulness of God? **4** By no means! Let God be true though every one were a liar, as it is written, "That you may be justified in your words, and prevail when you are judged."**5** But if our unrighteousness serves to show the righteousness of God, what shall we say? That God is unrighteous to inflict wrath on us? (I speak in a human way.) **6** By no means! For then how could God judge the world?**7** But if through my lie God's truth abounds to his glory, why am I still being condemned as a sinner?**8** And why not do evil that good may come?—as some people slanderously charge us with saying. Their condemnation is just.

Incidentally, the man I had hired to take charge of Marcon System Inc in my absence was the only man I ever knew, prior to Wrangell, who professed to be a serious and committed Christian. God's hand was in this as well. He was warning me about what I would later encounter. He was perhaps also giving me a lot of excuses I could later use to back out, if I were so inclined. Where was my heart? What will be the strength of my commitment? What or who is my commitment to? Of course, He knows the answers to all of these questions. But He needed for me to know the answers to those questions as well.

I appreciate C.S. Lewis' profound insight in this matter: "these same fanatic and homicidal Hebrews, and not the more enlightened peoples, again and again--for brief moments--reach a Christian level of spirituality. It is not that they are better or worse than the pagans, but that they are both better and worse." "It is great men, potential saints, not little men, who become merciless fanatics. Those who are readiest to die for a cause may easily become those who are readiest to kill for it. ... Of all bad men religious bad men are the worst. Of all created beings the wickedest is one who originally stood in the immediate presence of God."

Jesus himself left us a parable that perhaps reveals God's purposes in this. It is found in the book of Matthew, chapter 13, verses 24-30.

> **Mt 13:24 24** ... "The kingdom of heaven may be compared to a man who sowed good seed in his field, **25** but while his men were sleeping, his enemy came and sowed weeds among the wheat and went away. ... **30** Let both grow together until the harvest, ... Gather the weeds first and bind them in bundles to be burned, but gather the wheat into my barn.'"

All of this was an anathema to me in the light of all I knew and believed about God, and in the light of all that had drawn me to Him. It was perhaps my moment of 'unless you eat the flesh of the Son of Man and drink His blood, you have no life in you' (John 6:53) My response was quite similar to the response of Peter: "Lord, to whom shall we go? You have the words of eternal life." (John 6:68)That began my membership in the body of Christ. It has not been an easy relationship, but it seldom is.

anathema: a thing or person greatly detested.

The very people I sought so hard to avoid in my encounter with the pretenders among the business people of Bellevue, the unimaginative men and women who envisioned themselves to be the business and technology leaders, but were in reality drones, were dominate in the life of the church as well.

Within each church there are believers. Mixed in with these are often violent and blasphemous men, blatant drunks, loose women, and even sexual perverts, all struggling to overcome their handicaps. Among all of these are those who not only believe in God and Christ, but have completely dedicated their lives to that belief. Nearly all in the church profess to be believers in Christ. But few have committed themselves, their families, and their lives to living in accordance with that belief. Those represent the life of the church, which is Christ. These have given me hope.

In all of this, the hand of God is apparent. Will we choose to follow the great and powerful men and women of the denominational hierarchies, or the celebrities and 'anointed of God' of the TV and circuit ministries, or will we choose to follow Him and Him alone?

To those who look at the church and are turned off by what they see, I say, don't be dismayed. God is neither asleep nor helpless. Come join us! Help us to love the hypocrites in the church by showing them what faith is really about. The life of the church is in us. It is not in them.

My Faith

I am not a believer in or follower of church creeds and doctrines. I am a believer in God and in Jesus Christ His Son.

I am not Catholic, Protestant, Orthodox, Armenian, Methodist, Calvinist, Presbyterian, Baptist, Evangelical, Pentecostal, or a follower of any of the other denominational and sectarian movements. But I *am* a member of the church.

I am not a believer in the doctrines specific to a denomination or 'church,' where a doctrine is something we must 'believe' outside of God, and God's clear communication to mankind (i.e. the Word), to be an accepted member of that particular 'church,' denomination, or group.

I am not the scholar. I am a listener. I would much rather sit and listen at Jesus' feet, through His Spirit and through the Scriptures, than to be able to master all of the manuscripts, translations, commentaries, and systematic theology that the world has to offer. The hunger God has given me is a hunger to know and to worship Him, and Him alone.

My Journal
Selected Thoughts and Meditations

I have kept a journal for many years. It is a record of my life. But more than that, it is a tool I use in the formulation of my thoughts. In reading it one will find far more Scripture and personal meditations upon those Scriptures, than anything else. I desire that it, like the rest of my life and writings, be an open book.

If anyone ever wanted to get inside my head, which I do not recommend, for it is a very confusing and scary place, all they would need to do is delve into my journals. I have taken one short section of my journal and separated it out to make it less confusing, and decoded it to make it more readable.

I have provided selected journal entries in a separate booklet, *Meditations of an Alaskan*. This period covers the time leading up to when I began dealing with my cancer. I have provided selected journal entries covering the period following the discovery of my cancer in a second booklet *Meditations – April through August, 2012*. This covers the period from late April to the middle of August. I notice that two things differ from prior entries. The first is that politics is missing; the second is that the technical and literary sophistication are also gone. The loss of these has taken nothing away from the value of the journal.

I have broken out a separate record of select details of life on the 'backchannel' which I have titled *Mike's Logbook*. I have included these at the end of *Mike's Story*.

I have separated the remainder of this period of my journal into three separate parts, and have made them separate booklets: *Meditations in the Book of John*, *Meditations in the book of Romans*, and *Meditations in the epistles of John*.

My Calling
What Is My Calling?

What did God mean when He asked me to go along with what He is doing? He was certainly doing things both within me and external to me--through Leslie, Keith Buhner, and Rick (see *Wrangell, A Story of Redemption*).

Did God have full control over all of the circumstances? Yes. Did He exercise full control over all of the circumstances, or did He allow circumstances to develop within His will, and work through those circumstances and people (like me) to accomplish His will? There seems to be a place for both.

I don't seem to fit in anywhere within the church, that is within the denominational structures within the church, yet I also seem fit in everywhere outside of those structures, for those who are not exclusively married to those structures. I remember the Salvation Army's Captain Rick's shock in being confronted with a situation where, in the midst of our most controversial homeless ministry, one of the pillars of the community and of our church community, our lady doctor Harriet Schirmer, volunteered to come down and clean toilets. Jesus would have been, probably is, impressed.

God seems to be doing something different with me, and I don't pretend to know what it is. He has asked me to 'Go along with what He is doing and is about to do,' and I would not want it to be any other way. For one who is often considered to be a heretic, I have it really good.

Why was God willing to spend so much time, effort, and resources on me?

Since I have become a believer, a question has haunted me. What in the world was God doing spending so much time, effort, and resources in bringing me to the point where I could be saved? Or, what is in it for Him?

Many in the church take the position that God is desperately lonely, and will do anything to develop a loving relationship with us. Others take the position that He expends these efforts and resources in proportion to how much the individual is going to contribute to the Great Commission. I, for one, am one of the world's worst evangelists and all my desire and efforts to be otherwise have been to no avail. That is not my calling.

Others take the position that He expends these efforts and resources in proportion to the level of worship He expects to receive in return. Again, I, for one, a least publically, am one of the world's worst worshippers, and all my desire and efforts to be otherwise have been to no avail. In each case, God is supposedly doing something for us in exchange for what we will do for Him in return. Each, I believe, is a false ideology which assumes that, like us, does everything He does for selfish and self-serving purposes.

God has made it crystal clear to me, time and again, that none of what He is doing is of any benefit to Him at all. All His purposes, and all His efforts, are directed to our good and not to His own. There is absolutely nothing that we can add to or take away from Him.

My Goal

It is not my desire or my goal to win anyone over to my way of thinking or to my position. My goal, if there is one, is to encourage others, especially those outside of the church looking in, not to be distracted by the evil that is present in and often dominates the church, but rather to listen to God as He speaks through the life which does permeate the church—the children, and those with a broken heart and a contrite and humble spirit who tremble as He speaks, the seekers of God.

Only God Himself can draw someone to Himself.

There is some indication that some people are placed in this world who are destined by God, perhaps through their very nature, to become God's people. Others were given over to the devil to be planted by him, though we might not be able to tell the difference.

Yet still the offer of salvation is open to 'whomsoever.' It appears that some are destined to be His. Others will not be drawn by the Father, and will not be one of the 'whomsoevers.'

Is there also a category of people that receive an appeal by God, yet who choose the darkness over the light even so? Yet even these are destined before time to be lost to God's mercy.

He gave (gave up) His only begotten Son for an unworthy and undeserving people. That is sovereign grace. He did so that everyone who believes (is called and chosen to believe—which covers all options since God is sovereign) may not perish with the others (those of the world be adopted as sons, as brothers to Jesus Christ. To be baptized into His death is to enter together with Him into this death to all of the things of this world, and to the nature of this world, that we may be reborn in the Spirit and receive life together with and in Him as people of the Spirit and of the truth, as opposed to the people of the flesh and of the passions of the flesh that we have been. We are, instead, to be a people together with God, together with the Father and His Son.

There may be some indication in this when God sends his angels into the entire world to gather in everyone for the marriage supper of the Lamb. Within all of this there is the unmistakable warning that those who fail to accept Him, that is, to believe in Him, will perish with the world. Though He has called us (and them) He will not force Himself on us. We choose as a part of His sovereign will. This does not interfere with or take anything away from His sovereignty in all things. He has made us and knows us far better than we can know ourselves. He knows every hair on our heads. No sparrow (or person) falls to the ground without His knowledge. He knows who will make what decisions in life. As with me, one of the chiefs of sinners, He knew what my choices would be and when, what I would suffer, and what my response would be to Him when He called me. Though I was His from the very beginning of time, He allowed me to make the choices and mistakes that I did make, and allowed them to take place—to a limit. He didn't seem to be concerned about these, for He had much deeper issues to address and deal with in me.

Sometimes it feels as if God is just not there in my suffering. It seems that Jesus had had that experience on His cross, and Job as well. What is the purpose of suffering? 'He who has suffered in the flesh is done with sin.' What does this mean? Is it the end of pride, of self-centeredness, of selfishness? Or, am I still my own man in charge of my own destiny? It certainly makes me fully dependent upon Him and what He has in store for me, that is, unless I allow pain and suffering to drive me away from Him and turn to dependence on myself and upon the world and the devil our father. This is one of our choices—over our participation in His sovereignty.

Perhaps the one thing that my experience (cancer) has done is drive me closer to Him and full dependence upon Him, and upon His people as well.

Pictures

The Log Cabin

The old beach house

The new beach house and skiff

The beach where I camped
(under   the trees)

Mike and the old skiff and
the dugout

Mike and the dugout with
the 'fisherman's oar.'

Mike and the new skiff

Mike as a U.S. Marine

The Suskin family

KUENSTER

★ ★ ★

The president of Advanced Technology Laboratories, **Gordon B. Kuenster**, has been named vice president and a director of New York-based Squibb Corp., the large drug firm that recently acquired ATL, with headquarters in Bellevue.

The Bellevue company became a Squibb property after exceptional success in producing ultrasound diagnostic medical equipment. Kuenster joined ATL in 1977, after being logistics manager for the Boeing Co.

Gordon Kuenster

The Marcon Team

Two key players are not included in these pictures, they are Ralph and Sue Astengo. I apologize to them and to you for this. They were key to the whole affair. It was Ralph who carried the vision and got everything started. He served as president of ATL for the first ten years. Sue also played a key role in the very early days.

I also wanted to have a picture of Jim Pace, who was responsible for my move to Alaska, which is where this book begins. If there is ever a revised version of *Mike's Story*, I hope to include them.

Selected Wolf and Bear Encounters

One day, shortly after buying my float house and moving it up on the beach where I now live, I was out beach logging. As I was working, I returned to my stash for something and found large paw prints all around.

Later that afternoon I had returned home and was standing in the doorway of my cabin. A huge black wolf came out in front of my cabin and as he was crossing over to the other side he stopped and made his mark right in front of me. I whistled, and he completely ignored me, walking on and then going back into the woods on the other side of the float.

One night I was returning to my place at dusk. As I was coming out of the woods I could see two very large bears out on the point which forms the west side of the cove where I live. I stopped and waited until they moved on toward my place. When I did come out, they were only a little way down the beach and immediately detected my presence. Both stopped, and the larger of the two came back toward me while the other one waited. He stood and came right up to me, and sniffed me over. Apparently satisfied I wasn't a threat, he turned sideways, came down on all fours, rejoined the other bear, and they moved on toward my place. That was a very humbling experience. Whether I lived or died was completely in his 'hands.' He let me live.

Another day, I was placing posts for an outbuilding behind my cabin. I was lying on my stomach clearing loose dirt and debris out of the bottom of a post hole. When I got up it sounded like to entire woods was coming down on me. I turned to see a young (wild haired) brown bear a few feet away. He turned his head toward me and I could clearly see the complete road map of the red veins in his eyes. I thought - 'This guys going to see what a little piece of dung I am and is going to come back and swat me into eternity.' But no, he kept right on going, right over the top of the logs and pushed the stern of an old boat and the bushes and small trees out of his way. At this point it was quite comical.

The Angel Log

One day I was beach logging east of my place and had brought some logs out into the straight to catch the outgoing tide toward my cabin. A riptide caught them and carried them out into the middle of Eastern Passage, about a mile out, before I could catch up to them in my little 8' rowboat. There was one fairly large log (in girth) among them which was moving slower than the others. As I passed it on the way out I grumbled 'It sure would be nice if I didn't have to come all the back out and get that one.' Out of nowhere came 'Sure.' This was no epiphany, at least it was nothing like the others and I have never been sure what it was, but it was definitely supernatural. By the time I got the other logs back in and on the way toward my place it was dark.

When I got up the next morning I started watching for the log. I knew something happened and that something would happen, perhaps a current would carry it past, where I could go out and retrieve it, which would be no small matter in itself, considering the length and breadth of Eastern Passage. When it failed to show, I experienced a crisis in faith. Was I just nuts? No. It happened. Something is going on. I just don't understand what it is. This is the first (and only) time anything like this has ever happened to me.

Then I walked down off of the float and onto the beach to relieve myself. There was the log, setting up against the float within a foot of my tie up ring! That is the only log of that girth that has floated up on my beach by itself as long as I have lived there. The flow of the creek keeps such logs out.

The angel log is resting under two corrugated iron roofing panels at the East end of float.

An excerpt from my journal:

5-22-11 Sunday A log, the bottom half of a cottonwood tree, washed up on the beach in front of my cabin today. What is notable about this is that it is notable. This is the first time I can remember that a log doing this since the 'angel' log. The log is resting at about the half-tide level. The wind was blowing out of the northwest as I rowed home at 9:30 to 10pm. (The next day I discovered that this whole area has been inundated with parts of trees and logs which have been flushed out of the river and moved here by a powerful NW wind.)

Letters

A Christmas Letter

12-11-11 Sunday

Another year has gone by! I have been retired for 10 years. It amazes me how busy I still am. How do people find enough time to keep up with all there is to do, while working full time and perhaps even raising a family? My guess is that they (or perhaps you) can't.

I seem to have replaced my work-a-day routine with studies—of life (including its history), and of the world and universe in which we live.

I was once awed by the very size and complexity of the universe, and by the unfathomable principles upon which the universe exists and functions—its vast expansion in the realm of relativity to the incredible smallness of the quantum world— along with our insignificance within it all. I am still awed. At that time I found myself also confronted by fundamental questions, particularly 'why there is something rather than nothing,' which seems to violate a fundamental principle of the universe—which is that everything always seeks its simplest state. And, by what is life—does it have any importance, or purpose, or meaning? Do we need to deceive ourselves into thinking it does in order to not be consumed by nihilism? I viewed all attempts at addressing these questions through religion as merely the avoidance of dealing with them by succumbing to superstition.

If life has purpose or meaning, why do we insist on enslaving one another and butchering one another by the tens of millions? Why, on the individual level, do we spend all our time trying to satisfy our bodily desires, particularly our sexual desires, while at the same time trying vainly to add substance (wealth, power, fame, or legacy) to our meaningless lives?

What caught me totally by surprise (which seems to be the way God often reveals Himself to people) was something I never even considered—that notwithstanding all of this (even with the advent of the theories regarding the accelerating expansion of the universe, string theory, and multiverses today) there might be something far greater than any of and all of this, and that this gives being and life meaning. In considering this, and the incomprehensibility of what I already knew to be so, I could find no reason there might not be.

It took this being, who I now know as God, to make Himself and this known to me in a way that could not be denied. That He would bother to do this, with me, is another incredible part of it. I can now look up from insignificance to significance with a degree of awe which far exceeds the awe I once had for the universe and its workings alone. I now have time to contemplate all of this.

So, I have had a lot of catching up to do, and this by itself is enough to keep me busy. As a tool, I find journaling this helps me to gather my thoughts and findings together into some sort of order.

Then there is the weekly interdenominational fellowship and Bible study I have been asked to lead. It allows me to express some of my thoughts and questions, and much more importantly, to help provide a platform for all who are interested in sharing their thoughts, and difficulties, and blessings to do so. Then there are the other fellowship meetings—Sunday morning and sometimes Sunday night, Monday night, Wednesday night, and (Thursday morning), and sometimes Saturday morning.

This requires a whole lot of travel back and forth from my cabin to town (I haven't been able to get anyone to meet at my place).

This morning I am recuperating from bruises sustained leaving my bicycle in the dark yesterday morning. I hit an ice-ridge and became airborne. That wasn't so bad, but I knew sooner or later I would have to come down! And I did, sooner rather than later. Fortunately I had time stretch out and to position myself to absorb the impact and ended up with only a swollen elbow from coming down on a chunk of ice.

"Jesus declared, "I thank you, Father, Lord of heaven and earth, that you have hidden these things from the wise and understanding and revealed them to little children; yes, Father, for such was your gracious will. … no one knows the Son except the Father, and no one knows the Father except the Son and anyone to whom the Son chooses to reveal him. Come to me, all who labor and are heavy laden, and I will give you rest. Take my yoke upon you, and learn from me, for I am gentle and lowly in heart, and you will find rest for your souls. For my yoke is easy, and my burden is light." (Matthew chapter 11, verses 25-30)

Dear Rick and Sharon :
A Cancer Letter

On April 7th I participated in the Wrangell annual heath fair blood screening program. Three days later I was called into the clinic because of some disturbing results indicating my liver was not functioning properly. The doctor, DR. Greg Salard, had the hospital do an ultrasound scan of my liver and adjacent organs. Three days after that the results came in inconclusive. Dr Salard sent me in for a CT scan late that Friday afternoon. At 6pm that evening Dr. Salard gave me a call and I met him at the clinic. The CT scan showed an 8cm tumor in my liver that by all appearances is cancer.

The first thing the next Monday, Dr. Salard started the process of making arrangements to get me admitted into a hospital in Seattle or Anchorage. At 9:45am Tuesday Dr. Salard called. He had arranged for me to be checked into Virginia Mason that night and wanted me on the flight that day.

I left Wrangell at 4:30pm, arrived at Sea-Tac at 8:40pm, and took a taxi to Virginia Mason ER and checked in.

I was taken into surgery at 4:30pm that Thursday, to have stints installed to allow my liver to drain.

I was discharged from VM at 2pm the next day. My brother and his wife picked me up and took me tom their place. That Saturday afternoon my friend Jack on Camano Island picked me up and took me to his place so we could attend church together the following morning. That evening my condition began to deteriorate. At 2am Sunday morning I had my friend Jack drive me to Virginia Mason ER.

They admitted me and performed abdominal X Rays followed by another CT scan. The Health Team was concerned with my low pulse rate and blood pressure and had me taken down to the ICU.

The following Tuesday they redid the stints. This time they tried a new technique where they burn away the tissue forming a path through the tumor and then inserted metal stints in the channels. These stints usually last about a year. This method also gives the patients greater longevity.

The following Monday I was transported back into surgery and tubes were installed to drain the left side of my liver. Both stints were plugged. The drainage looked good and I felt much better. A few days later they redid this procedure (things get real fuzzy here). A few days after that they were able to plug the drain and remove the bag.

I am doing much better, gaining strength daily. I have a rare tubular cancer which was blocking my liver ducts. The liver is also involved. I now have two metal stints in channels which were burned through the tumors. All this was followed by serious infections which brought my blood pressure down to dangerous levels.

The doctors are trying to get me through a regime of antibiotics so that they can begin shrinking the tumor with chemotherapy. I will be in Virginia Mason until at least the seventeenth. We will see what happens then. The cancer is terminal. My care is palliative care.

I am extremely grateful for the time I have had with the Lord here on earth, and with His people. I am ready when He is.

Thanks for your prayers.

Mike's Logbook
(1-7-11 to 4-13-12)

I have put together a composite of portions the journal I have been keeping over the last several years. I have put together a composite of the record of interesting occurrences which occur on a daily and weekly basis when living and traveling in a remote area. I hope you will find these of interest. I have called them Mike's Logbook.

1-7-11 Friday
A fair sized surf was coming in from the NW all afternoon. The sky was clear. I left my cabin about 4pm during a lull in the surf, and just after sundown. It was a wild ride all the way. I was another clear night under the stars and a sliver of a moon. I could hear the surf breaking over the reefs as I passed outside of them. When I was finally inside the cove where my boat landing is, and was moving stern first into the landing area, an explosion of water erupted next to the boat, spraying me and starling me. I suspect it was a seal or sea lion, probably just surfacing, that went into a panic dive on seeing me.

I had little trouble riding in to town as the hard pack had solidified.

3-12-11 Saturday
A Slip on the Trail
It was a beautiful day with scattered snow showers. I left at 11:45 and hiked the trail to the road and from there up on the upper road. I started down from the rock pit toward my place but found myself in snow up to my waist. I retreated, and started back down the road. A father and his two boys came snowmobiling up as I descended. On the trail back to my cabin slipped and fell twice on the yellow line section. When I fell the second time I was unable to get up, for I could not gain a foot or hand hold. I had to use the line to pull myself back up on the ledge and then to the tree to which it was tied. If the line had not been there I wouldn't have been able to keep from sliding off the cliff and falling onto the rocks below and then into the water.

3-26-11 Saturday

When I got up this morning (quite late for I am quite sick) there were 5 ducks our front. When I appeared in the upstairs window, they came to full alert, except for one who had its head tucked under its wing taking a siesta. Shortly, one of the other ducks, on seeing this, charged full bore at the dozing duck rudely driving its beak into its side. The negligent duck came to full alert but they still stuck around alternately feeding and keeping a lookout.

After they paddled off, the two resident ravens appeared, squabbling with one another as always. With the way they treat each other one would expect them to separate, but, like an old married couple, they stick together like they were inseparable.

4-3-11 Sunday

It was windy and rough. Shortly after I arrived home, a humpback whale surfaced in the cove near the point—where I was rowing my boat but a short time before.

4-11-11 Monday

A yearling deer is grazing on the beach grass to the east of my cabin. It is watching a flock of crows scavenging small shellfish, fluttering up with them in their beaks, and dropping them on the rocks below to break them open. At one point the deer went back into the bushes, and then came bounding out scattering the flock of crows.

4-17-11 Sunday

As I was about to leave the porch, with oars under my left arm and buckets in hand, an otter came rambling up the beach. It was headed right for me, unaware of my presence. When it got about twenty feet from me I spoke softly to it. It stopped, looked at me, and then rambled back toward the water, ending up following the waterline west toward the creek.

The tide was extremely low (the net anchor was dry). On the way in (by boat) I came across a mink on the beach, at about the same place I encountered a mink swimming several days ago. I spoke to it and it stopped to get a good look at me as I rowed on.

4-20-11 Wednesday

I left the float-house at 9:13 and was abeam of Babbler Point at 9:46. A sea lion (one of a pair) welcomed me into the cove. The beach, even at low tide, was strewn with rocks and boulders all of the way into the cove. I found one small cockle on the surface of the point bordering the creek and unearthed one more. There were a few horse clams on the far reaches of the point. I took one (later dicing and freezing it.). There were hundreds of ducks in the mouth of Crittendon Creek. A dozen Canadian geese also came out. I left the mouth of the creek at 11am and arrived at the boat launch just after 12pm.

5-4-11 Wednesday

There is a raft of hundreds of ducks stretching from the beach out into the strait, moving in and out. A deer was feeding on the beach. Crows are dropping and breaking snails on the rocks, The two ravens are feeding on the pop-weed. Two herons are feeding in the shallows.

5-6-11 Friday

An eagle swooped down toward the ducks in the shallows, scattering them.

5-7-11 Saturday

A humpback whale cruised by the cove heading west and blowing once (that I saw). The rafts of ducks are no longer here. There is some wind and a mild chop. Flocks of duck are moving past.

5-8-11 Sunday

A raft of hundreds of ducks extended from the beach well out into the straight, just east of Dick's. They lifted off the water as I approached, moving further out. When I reached the place where they were sitting, startled ducks began popping up all around me. Perhaps a third of their number had been feeding below those who formed the raft on the surface. I learned something new here.

5-9-11 Monday

It is cloudy this morning. Huge flocks of ducks are moving past. A few are feeding in the shallows. A flock of shore birds--snipe?-- are moving as one body from one place to another, settling on the beach among the pop-weed.

A sea lion cruised by a little later.

5-13-11 Friday

Rafts of ducks are feeding in the cove and out into the straight. A mink is searching for food at the water line. The rafts seem to be following the feed. Small groups of ducks shuffle back and forth as individual rafts escalate into a feeding frenzy.

5-15-11 Sunday

I surprised a mink at the creek shortly after I arrived. It seemed to prefer to drown itself than confront me. It finally surfaced and fled up the other side of the creek.

5-23-11 Monday

The mink is wandering on the beach at the waterline. He was sunning himself on a rock there a few days ago, until he saw me and I saw him, and he casually swam toward the creek channel. A harbor porpoise was feeding out front. It is overcast and the water is dead calm.

6-1-11 Wednesday

Two young bucks passed by on the beach and headed up the game trail.

7am - A mink came down the stream bed again, checked out the beach below my cabin, then crossed the creek.

As I was launching my boat I looked up and saw what looked like a snow-white melon with two black dots that looked like eyes looking at me. When it submerged I knew it was a seal--an albino? It surfaced again as I was leaving. It was not an albino, but a seal with a white face.

6-22-11 Wednesday

On the way in an eagle was sitting on the point of the first reef and at least five others were in the trees overlooking it. The tide was nearing is apex. I saw signs of schools of small fish coming home the previous afternoon. Is this the smelt run?

7-13-11 Wednesday

An eagle spiraled down from the tall spruce trees on the East point and scooped something out of the water with its talons. He then landed on the beach causing the resident mink to scurry to safety in the tall grass.

10-15-11 Saturday

After my morning study, I gathered up my gear and headed for One Hour Island. A pod of Orcas passed me going the other way. I first heard and saw two cow Orcas, then a huge male surfaced. *Very* impressive! I watched them continue to surface and blow as they headed west.

I arrived at low tide and limbed the two trees, topped them, and then cut them away from the root wad—no problem. I cut each in two, 305" from the root wad and secured them with lines. Then I limbed the third tree. At high tide, I was unable to move the two out of the lower tide area. More work is needed. Once I get the two out of the tide as much as I can, and move the third to the tide, I plan to wait and move them on the higher tide at the end of the month.

10-24-11 Monday

After my morning devotions, I gathered my gear and took off in my 14' skiff for Hour Island. I had moved the free tree top out earlier and let it drift. I moved the two now floating tree bases out, tied them together with the large orange buoy, and let them drift while I retrieved the tree top. The second tree top is held by uncut branches. The sections of the 3rd. tree are as well. I lost track of the two base logs in the rain and mist as I was on my way to the beached tree top. I towed the tree top home. The outboard would run for awhile then quit. I believe water in the carburetor is the problem. (Tilting the engine up and then back down allows it to run a little longer.) After I got the log home I took the binoculars out to the point by Royce's and scanned the straight. I finally spotted orange and re-launched the boat and headed out. There were 3 to 4 foot waves cresting out where I ended up and where I spotted the orange again, so I kept going. I reached the buoy and couldn't tell whether it was one or two logs, and with much difficulty got a line on it. Then the motor quit again. I ran for short spurts a couple of times, but I ended up mostly rowing from about a half mile off the mainland to Wrangell Island where I tied the log off near Don and Bonnie's. It was a scary trip! Never again--not for firewood.

The waves out there had broken the line securing the logs together and on the way in broke the buoy line securing the buoy to the remaining log! I retrieved the buoy.

11-11-11 Friday
I launched the boat into a light surf, but then ran into high winds and breakers. It was two steps forward and on back as I bailed. At times I could make no progress at all.

11-12-11 Saturday
Last night I set my alarm for 3:30am and went to bed early so that I could make it to breakfast at Harbor Light in the morning. The wind howled all night. The water looked OK at 5:30am but the wind about blew me over on the way down the beach to check. Because of that and the rain, and poor visibility I took the trail. I had to climb through and over uprooted and broken trees that had come down during the night on the first part of the trail. Then I had to re-find the trail in the dark. A little further on, the first section of shelf at the top of the cliff (which forms the trail) had shifted down a couple of feet. It is now hanging by a few roots. I think this has something to do with why Dave Kyle calls it the death trail. The rest of the trip in went well. Those biscuits and gravy, with lots of Tabasco sauce, sure were good!

11-13-11 Sunday
It is Snowing! Kayla, Sydnie, and Andrew all ran to the windows and then outside to see the snow. They each had that special excitement that comes on children at the first sign of snow.

It was a beautiful night with a nearly full moon occasionally breaking through. It was an easy and pleasant ride and walk, until I came to a wall of fallen trees and rubble blocking my way. I couldn't find my way through and so headed up the steep embankment to find a way around it. I soon ran into a nearly vertical wall of solid rock, extending up as far as I could see. There appeared to be clearance right at the base of the wall but it consisted of a berm of loose dirt and mud. I thrust ahead and it held as I proceeded over the tangled mess until I could see the rope lines of the trail below. The weak section of the ledge which formed that part of the trail was still holding. When I reached the beach I came out into a beautiful moonlight scene. I was home at 9:15.

11-20-11 Sunday

The waves beyond Dick's were as large as I have seen them, but they were with me. The tide was fairly high and the reef provided protection for a landing on the west side.

12-15-11 Thursday

It is snowing.

It was still snowing. There was quite a bit of snow on the road but it was fluffy and easy to pass through. There was a strong east wind and white caps. I was able to launch my boat from behind the tip of the reef. It was a hard pull and progress was slow to past the 3/8 marker. It was sometimes difficult to hold my own against the high wind and waves.

1-20-12 Friday

It is snowing heavily.

There is 3-4 inches of snow. The wind was blowing out of the north. I almost decided to turn back when I hit the Spur Road and became bogged down in the snow. But once I got my snow techniques back I got into the spirit of it. The Spur Road was compacted enough by 4 wheelers and snow-mobiles to ride (barely). The water was far too rough to launch, but I really wanted to walk anyway. I met 4 wheelers and a snow board on Ballard Hill and past Ballard's.

I arrived home about 4:30. It was 25 deg. inside and out. The cabin was warm by 8:30.

1-22-12 Sunday

It is very dark and raining lightly. I had the seas behind me. I passed up my normal landing point and was able to come in behind a finger in the reef to make my landing. I walked to the main road pushing my bicycle through the slush (an hour walk). I arrived at Ted's just before 9am.

2-2-12 Thursday

The Spur Road was un-rideable because of the softness of the ice and the grooves in the ice. I launched into a pretty good surf. It was a hard row into the wind and the waves pretty much all of the way home. The porch was knocked of its supports, and logs and rounds scattered even though the highest tide since I left (Sunday) had been 14.7.

2-4-12 Saturday

Stars appeared during the night, with a sunset type of glow in the NE. clouds appeared to be obscuring the northern sky but when dawn arrived (just before 7am) the skies were clear. A light wind was coming out of the NW. it was just below freezing.

3-11-12 Sunday

It was snowing as I left for home. I launched the boat under the protection of the reef. A short while later I ran into as high winds as I have encountered. They were blowing me into the beach. I was barely able to keep it off the rocks. The wind slacked off and I made it OK. My porch was knocked off its foundation during the high tides, but all was OK. It snowed lightly overnight.

4-2-12 Monday

1:30pm – A whale jumped high out of the water about a mile out.

4- 10-12 Tuesday

11:30am Dr. Salard at clinic to review Health Fair results

My BUN number is high, indicating a failure of my liver function. My eyes are slightly jaundiced.

3pm Ultrasound exam. by Ann Cramer

4- 13-12 Friday

3:00pm CT Scan

At 5:50 Greg Salard gave me a call at Ted's, and I met him at the clinic. He inform me that the CT scan shows a 8cm tumor in my liver that by all appearances is cancer.

I am entering a new phase in my life. I have been living a very self-sufficient and independent life. I must now turn my body over to others, and eventually to the flames.

Wolf creek Mike, Eastern Passage,
Wrangell Island, Alaska.

wolfcreekmike@hotmail.com

© 2012 Wolf Creek Mike